Postcolonial Black British Theology

Dear Delroy,
Best wishes as you own writing.
Enjoy and engage with.
Michael.

TO Delroy,
keep on keeping on.
peace
Anth

Postcolonial Black British Theology

New Textures and Themes

Edited by

Michael N. Jagessar and
Anthony G. Reddie

 EPWORTH

Copyright © Michael N. Jagessar and Anthony G. Reddie 2007

The Authors have asserted their right under the
Copyright, Designs and Patents Act, 1988, to be identified
as the Authors of this Work

Scripture quotations are from the New Revised Standard Version
of the Bible, copyright 1989 by the Division of Christian
Education of the National Council of the Churches of Christ in
the USA. Used by permission. All rights reserved.

British Library Cataloguing in Publication data

A catalogue record for this book is available
from the British Library

978 0 7162 0626 2

First published in 2007
by Epworth
4 John Wesley Road
Werrington
Peterborough PE4 6ZP

Printed and bound in Great Britain by
William Clowes Ltd, Beccles, Suffolk

Contents

The Contributors

The Editors

Michael N. Jagessar holds a BA degree in theology, an MA in theology and Caribbean literature (both from the University of the West Indies) and a PhD in theology, ecumenism and missiology (University of Utrecht). He is a lecturer at the Queens Foundation for Ecumenical Theological Education. Dr Jagessar is co-editor (with Anthony G. Reddie) of *Black Theology in Britain: A Reader* (London: Equinox, 2007). He is also the Reviews Editor of *Black Theology: An International Journal*.

Anthony G. Reddie is a Research Fellow and Consultant in Black Theological Studies for the Methodist Church and the Queens Foundation for Ecumenical Theological Education in Birmingham. He holds a BA in (church) history and a PhD in education, and practical and contextual theology; both degrees conferred by the University of Birmingham. He is the author of a number of books, including *Nobodies to Somebodies* (Epworth, 2003), *Acting in Solidarity* (London: Darton, Longman & Todd, 2005), *Dramatizing Theologies* (Equinox, 2006) and *Black Theology in Transatlantic Dialogue* (Palgrave Macmillan, 2006). He is also the Editor of *Black Theology: An International Journal*.

David Isiorho completed his PhD research on the mode of involvement of Black Christians in the Church of England in 1998, at Bradford University where he was an Honorary Research Fellow. Dr Isiorho has worked as a parish priest in the inner city of Bradford and the former mining community of Brereton near Rugeley. He was responsible for racism awareness training in the diocese of Lichfield 1998–2000. He is currently vicar of the Parish Church of the Transfiguration, Kempston near Bedford. He is a member of the St Albans Diocesan Urban Forum and its Race Equality Committee.

David Joy is a lecturer in New Testament Studies at the United Theological College in Bangalore, India. He received his PhD in New Testament from the University of Birmingham in 2005. His thesis was entitled *Mark and the Subalterns: A Postcolonial Critique.* He is presently reworking his thesis for book publication in 2006/7.

Beresford Lewis holds an MA in systematic theology from Kings College London and is a PhD candidate at the University of Birmingham. His research is concerned with developing a political theology for Black majority churches in Britain.

Dulcie A. Dixon McKenzie is a PhD candidate in theo-musicology at the University of Birmingham. She is an experienced commentator on the gospel scene in Britain and hosts her own gospel radio show on Radio Leicester.

Delroy Reid-Salmon is the pastor of a 'Diasporan Caribbean Church' in New York (Grace Chapel). He holds a Master's degree in divinity from Harvard University Divinity School and also a PhD in theology from the University of Birmingham. His PhD thesis was on the theological identity of the diasporan Caribbean church.

Caroline Redfearn is a full-time doctoral student in the Department of Black Theology at the University of Birmingham, UK. She is funded by the Arts and Humanities Research Council and her area of study concerns the Black Church and inclusivity issues. After a 25-year career in child care, youth and community development in the UK, Jamaica and the Cayman Islands, she returned to England in the late 1990s to pursue academic study and theological training to enable the practical application of black theology to everyday life. She has an honours degree in sociology from Portsmouth Polytechnic (London External) and a MA with Distinction in Black Theology from the University of Birmingham. As a self-employed theologian and an ordained minister with the Metropolitan Community Church, she pastors 'black people's ministry in MCC' and an inclusive and affirming e-ministry, www.blackpeoplesministries.com for people of African-Caribbean descent, their friends and families. She lives by the sea in Bournemouth.

Carol Troupe is a research associate at the Queens Foundation for Ecumenical Theological Education. She holds an MPhil in education with theology from the University of Birmingham (2005). Her MPhil was entitled *The Contribution of Black Culture and Faith to Religious Education*.

Postcolonial Black British Theology: Introduction

Black theology in Britain

Black theology is a young discipline, but then in another sense, it is not. In terms of the latter, it should be noted that Black theology in Britain is as old as the contested nature of Black bodies in a country that has often defined itself in terms of homogeneity or sameness, based on notions of privileged and invisible Whiteness. Black theology as a self-named discipline and a radical form of Christian practice emerged in its more polished academic form in 1960s and 70s in the USA. It has grown out of the experiences of Black people of the African diaspora as they have sought to reinterpret the central ideas of Christianity in light of their experiences. However, Black theology is not simply a North American affair. If Black theology can be defined as the radical reinterpretation of the revelation of God in Christ, in light of the struggles and suffering of Black existence in order that dehumanized and oppressed Black people might see in God the basis for their liberation; then there has been a form of Black theology in operation in Britain since the epoch of slavery.

This text of postcolonial Black theologians emerges in the year we mark the 200th anniversary of the Act to abolish the slave trade in this country. Black theology in Britain can be traced, in many respects, to the pioneering work of Black abolitionists such as Equiano and Mary Prince in the eighteenth century. Black theology in Britain is not simply a new fad born out of a so-called postmodern age, built on the linguistic strictures of so-called 'political correctness'. Rather, since Roman times people have been speaking about God, and in doing so seeking to outline and determine the nature of their existence.

This text seeks to outline the newer and more recent developments of Black theology in Britain in the postmodern era, as highlighted principally by the growing proliferation of Black religious scholars and authors in this country.

And yet, in another sense, Black theology in Britain is very young. The first sole-authored book on Black theology in Britain was Robert Beckford's *Jesus is Dread* in 1998.[1] Beckford's piercing polemic was by no means the first such Black theology work in Britain. Prior to Beckford's emergence in the middle to late 1990s, the most significant Black theology texts in Britain – indeed the first to carry the nomenclature of 'Black theology' in the title – were two books edited by Raj Patel and Paul Grant: *A Time to Speak*[2] and *A Time to Act*.[3] Raj Patel is a Christian of South Asian descent and Paul Grant is a Black Christian sociologist. Both were connected with a grassroots Christian organization called 'Evangelical Christians for Racial Justice', based in Birmingham.

Despite the central importance of Robert Beckford's work, and the undoubted visibility he has accrued for the Black theology movement in Britain, it can be argued that the most significant development for Black theology in this country was the creation of the Black theology journal: *Black Theology in Britain: A Journal of Contextual Praxis*, which was launched on 10 October 1998 at the George Cadbury Hall in Selly Oak, Birmingham. A detailed investigation into the development of the journal has been undertaken by one of the co-authors of this text in a recent piece of work.[4]

In 2002 *Black Theology in Britain* became *Black Theology: An International Journal* and has continued to be the main conduit for the articulation and development of Black theology in Britain, if not the whole world. What has been most significant about the journal has been its unerring ability to combine the need for academic excellence alongside the continued commitment to nurture and foster new voices in this fledgling movement in Britain. In terms of the latter, many of the newer writers in this volume can attest to the support and encouragement they have received in the development of their scholarly work.

In many respects, this text is the latest development of the pioneering work of the journal. Many of the themes, theological concerns and the whole interdisciplinary nature of the Black theology journal are echoed in this text. The plural nature of the cast of players, the mixture of genders, methodological approaches and social location of the various authors is testament to the radical inclusivity of the Black theology journal and its development over the past several years.

Defining the term 'Black' in Black theology

When using the term 'Black' one needs to be aware of the multiple ways in which this term has been used within academic discourse in Britain. The word Black has to be understood within the context of Britain with all its peculiarities and inconsistencies. 'Black' does not simply refer to skin pigmentation, but is also making a political statement relating to one's sense of marginalization within the contested space that is Britain.

We use the term 'Black' in order to identify ourselves as a socially constructed 'other' when juxtaposed against the dominant Eurocentric discourses that dominate the normal picture and definition of what it means to be 'really' British.

This tradition of political mobilization around the once maligned and socially constructed term 'Black' has roots in the political left and the rise of coalition politics in the 1970s. The work of political activists and commentators such as Sivanandan[5] and Ramdin[6] has been supplemented by the work of primarily cultural theorists and postcolonial exponents such as Kobener Mercer,[7] R. S. Sugirtharajah,[8] and Stuart Hall.[9]

Con*

Introduction

Postcolonial Black theology in Britain emerges from the diasporan experiences of Black and Asian peoples and their experiences with and introduction to Christianity. For the bulk of mainly Caribbean people (who have historically constituted the development of Black theology in Britain) this emerging Christianity was one that sought to challenge the allegedly Christian inspired oppressive acts of White Imperial power.

The roots of a postcolonial Black theology lie in the counter-oppressive struggles of Black peoples in the Americas, the Caribbean, Asia and Britain to challenge the worst excesses of oppressive Christian-inspired supremacist practices through a radical reinterpretation of the central tenets of the Christian faith. This dialectical tension between White 'normalcy' and the Black subversive interpretative response can be found in the apposite words of John Wilkinson, who writes

> But the heart of Black Christianity lay not with the teaching of the white missionaries but with the form of Christianity which the slaves fashioned for themselves arising out of their *own* experience and needs.[10]

The roots of Black theology can be found in the radical and subversive reinterpretation of Christianity by Black slaves in the so-called New World, during the eighteenth and nineteenth centuries. Black people, having being exposed to the tendentious Christian education of the exploitative planter class in the Americas and the Caribbean began to 'steal away' from beneath the close confines of their slave masters to worship God in their own existential spaces.[11]

The desire of Black people to form their own ecclesial spaces was the process of a long period of history, arising from the 'Great Awakening' in the middle of the eighteenth century.[12] It is beyond the scope of this Introduction to mount a detailed analysis of the historical development of Black churches in the African Diaspora, but it is worth noting the importance of Black existential experience and context to the historical manifestation of such ecclesial bodies. Black theology begins with Black concrete experience of being human and not the historic mandates born of the often abstract philosophical musings as to the nature of God's being or some other obscure point of theological detail. Black Christianity, out of which Black theology has emerged, was born of the basic need to find some basis for proclaiming Black humanity.

[handwritten margin note: Theological anthropology]

The postmodern problem of invisibility

In April 2000, when David Ford's two-part article on 'British Theology' appeared in *The Christian Century* (2000),[13] Michael Jagessar recalled mentioning to the then editor of *Black Theology: An International Journal* the need to write a robust response to Ford's amazing silence and writing 'off' of Black British theology from his authoritative survey. That response never materialized. The third edition of David Ford's and Rachel Muers' *The Modern Theologians* (2005)[14] is yet to give Black British theology and theologians due recognition in terms of their place on the British theological scene. This may or may not be a deliberate strategy. It does, however, underscore for us that White British theologians are yet to grapple seriously with their theology, its relationship to the colonial and hegemonic agenda and what that relationship has done to their 'God-talk'. Such a scrutiny can begin right here at 'home' with a conversation with Black-British and Asian-British theologians. In the meantime, Black and Asian British theologians on these shores continue to 'do' and write theology as is reflected in the works of Robert Beckford, Mukti Barton, and Anthony Reddie, and through the international journal *Black Theology*.

In view of our continuing commitment to write theology from our own perspective(s), we launched an annual conference with a call for papers. The one-day conference, held on 14 July 2005 at the Queen's Foundation, Birmingham

elicited ten presentations[15] around the theme originally entitled 'Colouring Ministry'. These annual conferences are
intended to encourage more reflection and critical engagement in Black theological praxis, thinking and articulation
from a wider cross-section of Black practitioners, researchers
and scholars. It is also hoped that this initiative will contribute towards shaping some creative frameworks for doing
theology and practising ministry in our plural context(s) in
Britain. We hope that these conferences will be an ongoing
opportunity for Black and Asian scholars to present papers
on contemporary themes and critically defend them in a
scholarly space, and that their articulations can be published
to help the wider community of students and scholars both in
academia and pastoral ministry. This volume is the first in
what hopefully will be a continuing series of texts detailing
the development of Black theology in Britain.

Postcolonial Black theology

Why put 'postcolonial' in front of the words 'Black theology
in Britain'? What do we mean by 'postcolonial' and why this
insertion into Black British God-talk?

The notion 'postcolonial' is contentious in terms of the
multiplicity of ways it is used.[16] It is a term, position or
theory borrowed from literary studies and other disciplines
and it offers some exciting possibilities for God-talk and
religious discourse.[17] In the context of biblical studies R. S.
Sugirtharajah asserts that 'postcolonial' shelters a range of
distinct but related meanings. He writes

> First, in a historical sense, it encapsulates the social, politi-
> cal and cultural conditions of the current world order,
> bringing to the fore the cultural, political and economic
> facts of colonialism, and aiding the recognition of the
> ambiguities of decolonialization and the ongoing recolo-
> nialization. Secondly, as a critical discursive practice, post-
> colonial criticism has initiated arresting analyses of texts

and societies. It provides openings for oppositional readings, uncovers suppressed voices and, more pertinently, has as its foremost concern victims and their plight. It has not only interrogated colonial domination but has also offered viable critical alternatives. Thirdly, the term applies to the political and ideological stance of an interpreter who is engaged in anti-colonial and anti-globalizing theory and praxis. Applied to biblical studies, it seeks to uncover colonial designs in both biblical texts and their interpretation, and endeavours to read the text from such postcolonial concerns as identity, hybridity and diaspora.[18]

Hence, postcolonialism is not about the demise of colonialism as 'post' since it embodies both 'after' and 'beyond'. It is not about historical chronologies, but more about a critical stance, oppositional tactic or subversive reading strategy. We use the term 'postcolonial', borrowing from Christopher Duraisingh, to underscore 'a new mode of imagining, a new cultural logic, posited over against the eurocentric monologic and the colonial manner of thinking and visioning reality'.[19]

Now, this new mode of imaging or counter-discourse to the Eurocentric monologic has been at the heart of Black British theology from its inception. Black British theology's birth is tied to British colonialism and Black presence in Britain as a result of these encounters. Black theologians have been rereading and rewriting biblical/theological texts in the Empire's own frontyard. The implication is that Black British theology has been, in a number of ways, postcolonial from the inception. We therefore employ the term 'postcolonial' alongside Black British theology in the subtitle of this volume as a timely marker that links the past, present and future of Black theological discourse in Britain. There are, of course, other reasons for this juxtaposition.

Surgirtharajah correctly observes that

what is striking about systematic theology is the reluctance of its practitioners to address the relation between European colonialism and the field. There has been a marked hesitancy to critically evaluate the impact of the empire among systematic theologians, both during and after the European expansion. Theologians in the West cannot excuse themselves by suggesting that the empire had little impact 'at home'. New studies in literature, visual culture, geography and history in the last decade have demonstrated the numerous ways in which the empire was central to English domestic life and popular consciousness.[20]

Hence, our juxtaposition is affirmation of Sugirtharajah's observation, which is true of British theology. At the same time we are also keen to highlight Sugirtharajah's overlooking of the fact that Black theology in Britain has been a counter-theological discourse against the dominant White British theology – in effect the voicing and deploying of a postcolonial strategy without naming itself that way. The crucial point, however, is that postcolonial Black theology in Britain serves the purpose of differentiating itself from British theology as articulated by the dominant White group by taking the British plural context(s) with all its complexities seriously.

Given that the articulation of Black British theology was initiated by voices with Caribbean, African and Indian antecedents (from former colonial contexts), and given the complex and hybrid nature of the notion of Black in the UK context and the diverse views on what is Black theology, the term 'postcolonial' offers an appropriate way of understanding this complexity and the need to discern who is actually doing Black theology and at the same time it points to a significant dimension of Black British theological method, in the spirit of what Stuart Hall refers to as 'positionality'. For our purpose, this means that Black British theological discourse will seek 'to work reflexively',[21] open-endedly, rather than dwelling in exactitudes and fossilized dogmas. The eclectic nature of the essays in this volume points in this direction and can serve as an example and challenge for British theology in general to engage in the fresh configurations (as posited by Sugirtharajah in the foregoing extract).

A significant implication is the challenge that postcolonial presents to the internal dialogue within Black British theological discourse. For example, problematic is the fact that not every Black British Christian or individual group that claims a Black identity may be doing, thinking and writing Black theology or even want to associate itself with the Black British theological movement (BBTM). While Robert Beckford, for instance, writes from a Black Pentecostal tradition, that tradition as a whole will not associate itself with Beckford's theological discourse and its critique of them. Moreover, Beckford is just one voice within the BBTM. An equally prolific voice writing from one of the established church traditions (while critiquing it) is that of Anthony Reddie, the co-editor of this book. There are also other voices from historic church traditions that include Mukti Barton, Inderjit Bhogal, and Lorraine Dixon.

It is not insignificant that when White British theologians write on and attempt to evaluate Black theology in Britain they always take a myopic view by pointing only to Beckford's work. Is this because Beckford writes from a Black Pentecostal tradition and the White British theologians feel more comfortable to engage with the 'other' that is not Anglican or Methodist or the United Reformed Church? Or is it that such a myopic view merely reflects a strategy of not engaging with the Black voices from within the tradition of these 'White' colleagues? If so, it raises a bigger question as to their understanding of the history of their own tradition within which they are writing.

The essays in this volume challenge this mindset. Its eclectic and ecumenical nature in terms of gender, ecclesial traditions, theological positions and diversity of African/Black

British, Asian, Caribbean, Caribbean Diaspora voices further justifies our necessary and timely use of the term 'post-colonial'. It sharpens the necessary internal dialogue, underscores the intra-diversity and fluid nature of the discourse and will continue to plague the dominant British theology with the need for critical introspection: how is their theology shaped by British colonialism? And what has this done to them and their present inability to relate to the Black 'other' at home?

It is not insignificant that the postcolonial biblical discourse as articulated by Sugirtharajah, Musa Dube and Kwok Pui-lan (among others) exposes the central place of religious (and cultural) texts in the colonial/imperial mindset and agenda.[22] Given the Bible's central and sacrosanct role in Black British theological discourse and for the Black ecclesial traditions, the postcolonial gaze or scrutiny will unleash another challenge to Black British theological discourse. Together, we will need to grapple with our own designed unawareness of the role of (neo) colonialism in our inherited interpretive processes. Tough questions will need to be asked, answered and sides taken. For instance: how can the Bible and theological notions become relevant in the context of postcolonial Britain? Can we claim to be doing theology as Black theologians without taking off and scrutinizing our 'colonial' theological masks? In the process we will need to turn to appropriate heremeneutical/theological methods.

Black British theological discourse cannot be separated from Black Christian folks' need to articulate their faith and faithfulness geared towards giving agency to their experiences, identities, self-worth and empowerment. To borrow from the doyen of postcolonial biblical criticism, Sugirtharajah, postcolonial Black British theology's 'specific usefulness' will be in its continuing 'capacity to detect oppression, expose misrepresentation and to promote a fairer world rather than in its sophistry, precision and its erudite qualities as a critical tool'.[23] Postcolonialism as a strategic tool can serve to move Black British theological discourse beyond polarizations towards its liberating and transforming vocation.

The eclectic nature of this collection underscores not only the diversity and breadth within Black theology and Black religious discourse. It also highlights the danger of stereotyping Black God-talk and the necessity for continuing intra-dialogue and conversation. This is one reason why we want to play with the notion of 'Postcolonial Black Theology' in our title, as there is a multiplicity of perspectives of faith and spirituality in the lives of Black and Asian people in Britain. Our other motivation is primarily to underscore the challenges and possibilities that theology done from Black and Asian perspectives pose for the dominant monochrome theology that we call British and which largely excludes our experiences and stories.

Of equal import, for us, has been the desire to 'open out' the hinterland of Black theology in Britain, removing it from the essentialized discourse that wants to locate the ongoing development of this discipline purely within the perspective of Pentecostalism or the seemingly narrow prism of so-called 'Black-led Churches'. This book not only plays with the notion of 'postcolonial' it also offers a multiplicity of paradigms by which we might conceive the nature, intent and direction of Black theology. The authors, from a variety of backgrounds, offer perspectives that are at once within the Church, adjacent to the Church and in some respects, significantly beyond it.

We hope that in reading these chapters individually and as a corpus, readers will catch a glimpse or experience a taste of some of the present and future direction of Black theology in Britain. So this book is a challenge to both the macro, White-dominated terrain of generic British theology in addition to posing hard questions for the micro, Black-dominated hinterland of Black theology in Britain. In terms of the larger, more macro concerns, Black theology in Britain is casually disregarded or perceived in a very limited manner, whether from the likes of Ford and Muers (ignoring Black theology in

Britain altogether) or from Kee, who aside from confidently declaring Black theology dead also believes that this movement is reducible to one person; namely Robert Beckford.[24]

This book challenges the more macro terrain of White British theology to take Black theology in Britain seriously. As we have stated previously, the editors have noted the ways in which theology in Britain remains a most studiously White affair in a manner that cannot be said of other disciplines such as sociology and cultural studies. Aside from casual patrician arrogance of producing an overarching text that totally ignores the Black British presence (we are reminded of Paul Gilroy's great maxim 'There ain't no Black in the Union Jack'[25]), this form of scholarly myopia ignores the radical growth of Black Christianity in Britain. When religious commentators speak of Christianity in Britain dying or changing irrevocably,[26] they rarely factor in the growth and expansion of Black Christianity in Britain and the way in which this movement in potentially redefining the nature and intent of British Christianity and the Church in the UK.

The portents of gloom are predicated on the notion that Whiteness and the concerns of White people are the only factors that are essentially of any import in this nation. If one seriously engaged with the legitimate claims of Black theology in Britain, then anthologies and religio-cultural commentary would look and read very differently.

But of equal import, to our minds, is the necessity for Black theology in Britain to acknowledge its plural, ancestral roots and diasporan geographical routes. As we have stated previously (and restated here for added emphasis) there has been a tendency within Black British Christianity to presuppose a normative Black-led Pentecostal gaze to the development of Black theology in Britain. Reddie's previous work has shown the erroneous nature of this assumption and contention.[27]

In developing this collection, the authors have sought to demonstrate the eclectic and plural nature of Black theology in Britain – a postcolonial Black theology. The chapters each speak to a form of 'catholicity' that now exists in the movement. The editors – who also serve as Reviews Editor and Editor respectively of the Black theology journal and are also leading figures in the main Black theology in Britain Forum, which meets at the Queens Foundation in Birmingham – have sought to create and compile a work that recognizes the broad range of approaches and perspectives that exist in Black theology in this country.

The authors who spoke at that initial conference in 2005[28] and whose work is featured in this text, were all, at the time of writing, regular attenders of the national Black Theology Forum, which has always been an eclectic and plural space, limited only in terms of not allowing White people to attend.[29]

You will note that the various authors straddle multiple ethnicities, geographical locations, methodological approaches and theological perspectives. While Reddie's work is concerned with theological method (see his previous *Dramatizing Theologies*[30]), the chapter by David Joy is concerned with hermeneutics in India (reflecting the postcolonial context of the UK), Caroline Redfearn addresses the long-suppressed issue of human sexuality and its relationship to Black people in the African Diaspora and others, such as Delroy Reid-Salmon are interested in questions of diaspora. We mention these particular pieces not to privilege some voices at the expense of others, but simply to highlight the eclectic nature of this volume.

Our guiding principle in compiling this collection from the fruits of an exciting and vibrant conference is to offer a significant challenge to the overarching White mainstream and the more micro world of Black Christianity in Britain[31] in general and Black theology in particular. This text is significant for the plural and dynamic articulation of Black theology it offers for postcolonial twenty-first-century Britain. In many respects, its catholicity is more representative of Patel and Grant's *Time to Speak* and *A Time to Act* than the later, more famous work of Robert Beckford. This does not seek to devalue or disregard Beckford's epoch-defining work; but rather, seeks to articulate the breadth of ecclesial, ethnic, theological, educational, geographical and gendered plurality that is postcolonial Black theology in Britain.

The chapters in this book

Anthony G. Reddie's chapter, 'An Interactive Methodology for Doing Black Theology', utilizes drama as a means of creating a participative approach to undertaking Black theology. Reddie outlines a participative methodology that attempts to reconcile the perceived wide chasm between academic Black liberation theology and church-orientated folk theology. This method for undertaking Black theology is one that attempts to reconcile the more explicit political theology of systematic theologians with an appreciative pastoral perspective often employed by practical theologians when engaging with those at the grassroots in local churches. This approach is one that adopts a 'diunital' mode of operation in order to hold together entities that often seem in tension and which are viewed by many as being oppositional.

Carol Troupe's chapter, 'The Role of Black Theology within Secular and Plural Contexts', attempts to take Black theology into a new context. Such a new context necessarily address secular and religious concerns of the Black people who are subjected to those conflicts in their milieu. Troupe examines the issues surrounding the development of a religious education resource that incorporates the experiences, cultures and histories of Black communities into teaching about Christianity in schools. The paper is a ground-breaking attempt to take Black theology into the 'secular' classrooms with a view to making a difference to the education of young people.

Dulcie A. Dixon McKenzie's chapter on 'Black British Theology in Gospel Music' is like that significant intermezzo inserted between acts of a play. It is an eye-opener for many in terms of understanding the origin and growth of Black British Gospel music. Though she feels that most of the songs and their patterns are adopted from the United States Black Gospel music, she emphasizes certain original elements in the music. She laments, however, that at the same time the British Black Gospel music has lost its roots and makes a case for unearthing and reclaiming it.

Beresford Lewis in his chapter, 'The Letter Kills but the Spirit Gives Life', presents a number of concerns about evangelism, mission and culture. He proposes a method of dialogical relationship and celebration to bridge the gap between different communities and denomination and age groups. This will lead the communities to survive with a sense of identity and culture.

David Joy, writing from a North Indian context and as a traveller in the UK for three years doing biblical studies research, reflects on 'Images of Ministry: A Postcolonial Rereading'. He argues that some of the images or ideas such as 'kingdom of God', 'grace' and others have been mis-interpreted by theologians during the colonial era for their political and religious convenience while neglecting their original meaning. He also raises questions about the fruitful-ness of hermeneutics in a postcolonial period depending on the experiences of suffering of the people. The present state of Indian Christian theology is also analysed in the light of colonial and neo-colonial conditions of the people.

David Isiorho's chapter looks at the Church of England – the established church in England. The author writes as an insider (he is an Anglican priest) in his exploration of the links between Englishness, invisible 'White' ethnic identity and the Anglican Church in Britain. Isiorho argues that the seemingly invisible construct that is Whiteness is an impor-tant emblematic feature of how the Church of England configures itself in terms of its own self-identity. This con-struct is predicated on White normality, privilege and the preservation of White elite cultural norms. Isiorho uses the substantive ideas of Black theology to critique this barely acknowledged construct in order to unmask Whiteness and to open a conversation as to how the cultures and identities of Black peoples can inform and potentially redefine the meaning of the Church of England. In effect, Isiorho is offering us a nascent Anglican Black theology of liberation for the UK.

Writing from a Caribbean Diaspora context, Delroy A. Reid-Salmon's input entitled 'Out of Every Tribe and Nation: The Making of the Caribbean Diasporan Church' opens a number of issues on the identity of the Caribbean Diaspora Church. As diasporan identity and existence are highly problematic issues, it is important to pay attention to every aspect of the socio-political contexts of the people. Reid-Salmon contends that the diaspora people always come across three main issues, namely origin, community and racism, and that in rereading these issues the geographical context is significant.

Caroline Redfearn's chapter is part of a larger research project with the working title 'The Nature of Homophobia in the Black Church and the Movement towards Inclusivity'. Redfearn's chapter is not a theological text as such, but rather provides some invaluable research as to the historical, socio-political and cultural issues that have helped frame the submerged and hostile responses to issues of homosexuality within many Black churches in Britain. This is a groundbreaking piece of work in progress, some of the first fruits of which are to be found in this text.

Michael N. Jagessar's chapter, 'Spinning Theology: Trickster, Texts and Theology', concludes this collection. A member of the Caribbean diaspora, Jagessar draws on the Caribbean patron saint, Anancy, as a conversation partner in doing and articulating theology in a different way. Anancy's limbo-dancing theologizing, contends Jagessar, offers ripe possibilities to open up creative spaces to break through our rigidity and unnecessary theological polarizations. Anancy discourses do not pretend to give quick answers to our complex lives and contexts. They will merely highlight the sharp, contradictory and complex nature of faith and faithfulness and the need for a multiverse approach to theologizing.

We trust that you will enjoy the many colours and textures of this new anthology of Black British theological work in Britain. The multicolour of the margins continues to challenge the monochrome Whiteness of the centre. *Postcolonial Black British Theology* is an important first for this context!

Michael N. Jagessar and Anthony G. Reddie

Queens Foundation, Birmingham

The lines of Black Theology are becoming blurred

1. An Interactive Methodology for Doing Black Theology

ANTHONY G. REDDIE

Introduction

Within the context of this study, particular attention has been given to the efficacy of attempting to work in a participatory manner. There has been much written on the importance of critical, shared reflection as a means of doing theology.[1] I am also cognisant of the literature, which while supportive of the general tenure of Black/liberationist approaches to pedagogy and learning, seeks to problematize and critique many of the basic assumptions of these approaches to participatory reflection. Can a more inclusive and participatory approach to doing theology cope with the often complex ways in which Black people express themselves, particularly in contexts that are deemed not 'safe' or in which they do not feel comfortable?

Using a participation observational model for engaging with the voiceless

In order to engage with those whom I will term the voiceless, in a manner that would emphasize their autonomy and subjectivity, it was essential that a theoretical and practical framework be found, which would foster consistent 'truth-telling'. I was unconvinced of the efficacy of traditional theological discourse in this regard. It is interesting to note the general drift in Black theology among what might be termed 'Third Generation' Black scholars. The emphasis has moved from doctrinal or systematic concerns to more inter-disciplinary avenues, often risking the charge of being merely self-indulgent entertainment for its own sake, shorn of the need to engage with the contextual needs of a wider community.

The work of Pinn,[2] Dyson[3] and Beckford,[4] for example, has alighted on the area of Black popular culture as an arena for pursuing Black theological discourse. Influenced by these scholars, and more latterly, by the work of Thomas,[5] I have chosen to use the arena of ethnography and participant observation as a means for distilling the issues and concerns of Black people. This method of interrogating Black experience enabled me to gain valuable insights into the world of the voiceless, so that I could then create critical dramatic pieces that would become the conduit for a theology for those without a voice.

Participant observation is viewed as a distinct and impor-tant element within the wider area of ethnographic study. It requires that researchers engage with the ongoing life experi-ences of the people that they are attempting to study. While the philosophical roots of participant observation are to be found in social anthropology, the origins for the practical application of this discipline lie in the Chicago school of social research in the 1920s and 1930s. This rise of observa-tional research in Chicago led to a whole arena of study that found expression in diverse social and cultural milieux such as criminology, 'race', and urban studies.[6]

The importance of participant observation as a method-ological tool has been charted by, among others, William Whyte. Over a prolonged period, utilizing this method in a variety of contexts, Whyte attests to the efficacy and contri-bution of participant observation to social scientific research.[7]

A number of anthropologists, cultural and literary theo-rists, sociologists and researchers have found that the seem-ingly simple art of observation is a very grave misnomer. Writers such as Hammersley,[8] Glaser and Strauss,[9] Pryce,[10]

Bryman[11] and Silverman[12] have commented on the complexities of researchers observing social situations. Concerns that arise from this literature surround the conceit and deceit in the theoretical assumptions of the observer in relaying their perceptions of what might be termed 'observed reality'.

Putting ethnography to work in the service of the voiceless

My hope in utilizing the method of participant observation is to enable a more critical and honest assessment of the religio-cultural context and experience that has shaped and continues to influence the subjective selfhood of Black people. How does being (for the most part) poor, Black and without influence or positive visibility affect one's immediate outlook in postcolonial Britain? Black cultures and the cultural production that arises from this phenomenon have proved vital tools in the ongoing work of Black religious scholars.[13]

What I propose to do in this section of the study is to use the overarching framework of ethnography and participant observation, to reflect on and analyse the socio-cultural and religious context of voiceless Black people in Britain. This analysis will serve as the backdrop to my ongoing attempts to create an approach to doing theology in partnership with the voiceless through the medium of drama. I hope to draw upon the insights of educationists, cultural theorists and developmental psychologists to assist me in this analysis.

Postmodern game playing

The challenge to distil accurately the central characteristics and features that inform the experience of any community has been documented in the previous section on participant observation. Much of the aforementioned discourse has been my understanding of some of the literature pertaining to the overarching methodology of ethnography. If I wanted to work alongside Black voiceless people in an act of solidarity, it was imperative that I devise a means of making the fruits of the aforementioned discourse more accessible in order that these people can assess its veracity for themselves.

In a previous piece of ethnographic research, I investigated the whole area of Christian education and nurture of African Caribbean children in inner-city churches in Birmingham.[14] At a mid-point in the research, I analysed a number of religio-cultural festivals in the differing churches. I was interested to see how these churches celebrated 'Harvest Festival' and to what extent Black religious and cultural expressions of faith were in evidence within these settings. On one occasion, I was amazed to find myself in a Black majority setting with a number of Black young people, trying to participate in a very traditional barn dance. The idea of Black people engaging in a barn dance intrigued me. Constraints of time prevent any significant description or definition of a barn dance. Some have described the barn dance (sometimes called a Ceilidh) as 'a collection of dances which can be done by anyone who can walk, and knows their left from their right hand! The dances are usually fairly straight forward and can be learnt on the night of the dance with the help of the caller. No previous knowledge is required.'[15] Barn dances have their origins deep within the folk culture of village life in England, and in other parts of the world, particularly, North America. Observing these Black young people smiling at the sight of their parents and grandparents attempting to join their White peers in learning the steps to a traditional White (British) cultural practice implanted in my mind an idea that would assist me many years later. Why not combine the insights of ethnography with an experiential learning model based upon an imaginary construct – namely a barn dance?

Constructing the imaginary barn dance

Working with three groups of Black young people in London (although I have used only the reflections from one group for this section of the research[16]), I invited the various participants to construct an imaginary barn dance. Group 1 consisted of eight Black young people, between the ages of 18 and 21. All the participants were born in Britain. Five of the group were male and three were female. Of the eight participants, five had grandparents who were born in the Caribbean. The other three were born in Africa. The parents of these young people were, for the most part, born in Britain (six of the eight). All group participants belonged to a Black majority church of some form (Church of God of Prophecy, New Testament Church of God, Adventist, Methodist, Anglican and the Baptist Church).

I met with the group on three occasions. The task I set them was to make an exhaustive list of the various approaches one would undertake in order to 'discover the truth' of the barn dance. What approaches would enable them to learn the central features and issues at play in this fictitious barn dance? What were the different ways one might interrogate the reality of the barn dance?

The only rules for undertaking this exercise in self-actualization, was that the young people should imagine themselves as being present at the barn dance, both as a participant and an observer. This thought, quite naturally generated a good deal of levity, as many of the young people could not imagine themselves ever attending a 'dry' event like a barn dance.

The various group members were encouraged to adopt the position as the 'critical friend' at this imaginary event. Their presence was to join in imaginatively with the whole phenomenon of the event. They should dance and interact with the imaginary others, but juxtaposed with this participation, was the critical element of observation. In their capacity as participant and observer, what questions would come to mind? What would emerge from their engagement with others in the barn dance?

What was most impressive about this exercise was the means by which the group quickly became aware of the metaphorical basis of this imaginary construct. Clearly, we *were not talking about a barn dance per se.* The group saw the barn dance as a metaphor for church, or in more macro terms, Black people in Britain as a whole.

In order to explore these ideas further, I asked the various individuals to reflect upon the imaginary barn dance, with particular emphasis being placed upon those questions that seemed most intriguing or relevant to them. Which of the various points raised in their previous discussions were the most important?

The young people were mainly concerned with issues of 'style and interpretation'. There appeared less concern with the particular factual elements of the dance, such as the history or the development of the event. What concerned the group to a much greater extent, were those questions pertaining to how the dance was constructed, and who got to decide what style of music or moves were permitted at this cultural event.

My intention in devising this exercise was to see whether, by using the method of participant observation in an imaginative, dramatic form, one might enable these young people to interrogate their reality more critically. I was not concerned, to any great extent, with the content of their responses.[17] Rather, I wanted to assess the process of thought that might emerge from this exercise. In what ways did this exercise, which incorporated many of the salient features of participant observation, enable these young participants to reflect upon aspects of their own culture and identity?

In using this creative and dramatic device, I wanted to create a form of affective dissonance between the subject and the wider cultural environment. Previous research with Black young people had alerted me to the fact that learnt behaviour and the strictures of religious socialization often create a level of inhibition and constricted thought in any resulting discourse arising from the encounter with a researcher.[18] In short, people learn the correct language and terms to use, which often leads to an ability to speak a more explicit truth arising from experience.

In using this device, it was my hope that these Black young people would be enabled, through a distancing process, critically to engage with their wider environment and context. The semantic 'game playing' was very much embedded within the framework of the exercise. As the young people began to imagine themselves dancing and participating in this barn dance, they realized instinctively that this exercise was both real and imaginary. The exercise was both about the barn dance and concerned with greater issues external to this event.

This sense of a dialectical consciousness is a staple ingredient of a number of approaches within practical theology. It can be seen in the work of Jerome Berryman and his approach to undertaking theological reflection with young children,[19] or the Womanist-inspired pedagogy of Lynne Westfield.[20] In both schemas, the ability to hold two competing notions of truth dialectically, and allow them to interplay with each other, is central to the methodology of their work.

The fact that these Black young people were very much concerned with the style and interpretation of the dance calls to mind the research of Janice Hale-Benson and her pioneering work into the learning styles of Black children in the US.[21] She argues that one of the characteristic features of the learning styles of Black children is their ability to improvise and create new meaning from established norms or templates, rather than attempting to replicate those existing patterns.[22] These young people were not overly concerned with the possible rules of engagement within this imaginary construct. Rather, their primary interest lay in how they might express themselves within this cultural context. Particular emphasis was given to the covert or implicit rules within the barn dance. How could one know if what was stated about this phenomenon was the whole truth? What if 'certain people in power were chatting long talk (empty rhetoric), simply hiding their true motives?' This theme became a recurring one in the final section of the three meetings. How could we know the truth of any situation? Would we recognize the truth if and when it confronted us?

The contemporary resonance of this discourse for the religious and theological sensibilities of the various participants was stark and self-evident. A number of participants spoke of the restricted nature of their church and the limitations imposed upon them by church leadership often out of touch with the needs of young people. The suspicion levelled at ecclesial authority echoes the much vaunted 'hermeneutic of suspicion', based on commonsense experience that is at the heart of Black theological discourse.[23] In the words of one of the group participants, 'Just because they say it goes like that, doesn't mean to say, it has to go like that!'

Issues arising from the exercise

Among the number of factors that emerged from this exercise was the sense that these young people were enabled to reinterpret their reality by means of a distanced, yet engaged dramatic metaphor. Upon the conclusion of the second of three sets of meetings, I ask the group to identify a central theme or concern around which I could write a drama that might explore these issues.

After a great deal of conversation and hilarity, it was felt that the issue that most came to mind was that of 'truth telling'. Can people be trusted when they make particular pronouncements? Is it not the case that 'everyone has something to hide?' Further discussion led the group to consider the life and ministry of Jesus. Could he be trusted? Were his motives clear and unambiguous?

In the midst of this ongoing discussion, I was at pains to remind myself of the disparity between myself and my research subjects. I was a male academic in my late 30s. There was an age-gap of some 20 years between this group and myself, and a significant gulf in our social status. I am a recognized scholar within my church and the theological institution in which I work. These young people were largely anonymous. Five of the group were unemployed. Two members of the group were at university, with large overdrafts from the bank and no certainty as to their future employment. Another individual was working for the local authority. It was his first job, and he was 21 years old.

I was conscious of the tendency among Black people to 'signify' when in the company of authority figures. Beckford describes signifying as:

> The ways in which African Caribbean cultures 'play', 'manoeuvre' and 'conjure' a subject, issue or event so as to arrive at 'direction through indirection'. Signifying can be a form of trickery that enables oppressed people to negotiate or manipulate the dominant power.[24]

Given the tendency of Black people to signify, I was determined to exercise some caution in terms of the discourse that emerged from my encounters with the group. Might they be guilty of telling me what I wanted to hear? The challenges of engaging with this group of largely voiceless Black young people (very much reminding me of myself when I was their age) were very real and clearly apparent. As a Black religious scholar, was I working at the behest of their church leaders, in order to convince them of the efficacy of attending church and believing in God in a more orthodox manner? My assurances that I was working independently were largely heeded, but to what extent they were internalized and believed is a moot point.

Listening to and critiquing the voices of the voiceless

Utilizing the framework of ethnography and participant observation, I was able to devise a means of enabling young, voiceless Black people to reflect upon aspects of their experience. This process was achieved by constructing an experiential, participatory activity in which these subjects were at once distanced from, but yet connected to, their ongoing reality by means of this extended metaphor.

I have mentioned the habitual facet of signifying within Black cultural life. To what extent can any discourse by Black subjects (when confronted by authority figures) be entirely trusted? The ways in which Black people 'play' with reality, often invoking metaphysical elements, such as the 'spirit', creates very real tensions for the researcher.[25] For many Black people, their general theism and theology enables them to hold a dialectical perspective on reality. The concrete and explicit is not all there is. According to Theophus Smith, one of the means by which African Americans play with reality is through a process he terms 'conjure'.[26] Conjure is the practice of magic by which one is referring to the manipulation of one's environment in order to overcome the laws of nature for the purpose of effecting a semblance of change for the benefit of oneself and the disadvantage of another.[27] Reflecting on Smith's work, Frederick Ware states:

> Smith makes clear that African Americans are not the only group who use magic. Non-Americans in Western civilization also use conjure, and so he believes magic or conjure is a suitable category for the study of not only African American religion but the religion of other groups seeking empowerment.[28]

Ware's assessment of the generic qualities of conjure within Black religious traditions and sensibilities call to mind the work of such scholars as Albert Raboteau[29] and Robert Hood,[30] both of whom have investigated the religious traditions of Black people of the African diaspora. Their work is characterized by a pervasive sense of the work of the spirit(s) within Black life. The spirit offers alternative ways of knowing,[31] and provides an alternative, parallel reality to the concrete nature of the immediate built environment that most commonly confronts us.[32]

I am aware of the tension within Black religious and theological discourse surrounding the relationship between the spirits and the Holy Spirit. The latter is contained within a distinct Christian framework that is often seen as being an anathema to or simply distinct and separate from the former.[33] Recent ethnographic research, in Africa for example, is beginning to tease out some of the complexities of this discourse.[34]

As I have stated in a previous publication, when working with Black elders in Birmingham,

> For Black elders, the secular and the religious meet and co-exist in the one time and space. The 'here and now' and the 'hereafter' exist in the one continuum. The spirit world and the material world meet . . . Theirs is a world of miracles and the ordinary – often, miracles within the ordinary, a world of the spirit and the flesh.[35]

This dichotomized and dualistic perspective in Black experience and ontology, often the result of a deep-seated, inherent religious consciousness offers very real challenges and opportunities for the religious educator and theologian. The challenges arise from the difficulty of taking any Black discourse at face value. Within the generic, non-confessional arena of country schools in the UK, for example, Christine Callender notes the role of signifying within the broader linguistic and cultural repertoire of Black children and young people.[36]

The challenge of moving beyond the façade of Black discourse means that no researcher can take what they hear or observe at face value. The penetration of Black subjectivity requires a depth of analysis that engages with the multi-dimensional nature of Black religious and cultural expression.[37] This form of analysis constantly asks questions of the subject and the wider environment in which they are housed.

This complex nature of Black subjectivity requires that the

scholar/researcher (whether religious or otherwise) adopt the role of the 'critical friend'. The position is that of the slightly distanced participant and observer. One needs to maintain a critical distance between oneself and the subjects with whom one is engaging. That distance has to be carefully realized, for if one is too far removed from the experiential realities of the Black subject, the facility of signifying or the subordinate elements of 'cultural dissonance' will leave the scholar floundering in a cultural vacuum.[38] Cultural dissonance in a Black postcolonial experience in Britain

> manifests itself in a wide variety of social settings. Cultural dissonance is felt when one feels out of place in a cultural setting that is different from one's own. For instance, a Black person feels at home where Black traditions, values, belief systems and practices are the norm, and feels cultural dissonance in the wider socio-political environment where White, Eurocentric norms hold sway.[39]

I have written in the past on the difficulty of White authority figures gaining access to the inner lives and subterranean subjectivity of Black people due to the ongoing issues of signifying and cultural dissonance.[40] In effect, in order to work alongside and in authentic solidarity with the voiceless, one needs to engage in a delicate balancing act of not being too close or distant from those with whom one is hoping to engage.

The role of the slightly distanced participant and observer requires a commitment to multi-dimensional analysis. This form of analysis does not seek to simply gain access and interrogate the discourse of the Black subject (the voiceless). Juxtaposed with the analysis of the subject, is the necessity of critically reflecting upon the wider context in which the Black self is housed.

The development of liberation theology has provided the much needed methodological underpinning for this form of structural, situational analysis. Structural, situational analy-

sis seeks to place the experiences of the individual or community into a larger contextual framework, in order to shed
light on the issues and factors that are exerting an adverse
effect upon the selfhood of the oppressed.[41]

On both sides of the Atlantic, a new generation of Black
theologians has begun to reappropriate the work of Juan
Luis Segundo and his method for contextual theological
analysis. In the United States, Harry Singleton has attempted
to unite the differing but complimentary works of James
Cone and Segundo, in order to discern the most appropriate
method of doing theology in light of the ongoing oppression
of the poor and people of colour.[42]

Within the British context, Robert Beckford employs
Segundo's method in order to create a contextual theological
framework for addressing gang violence and gun crime in
Britain.[43] I have utilized ethnography and participant observation in order to gain access to the complex subjectivity of
the voiceless. This internalized form of socio-cultural analysis has been juxtaposed with the situational analysis of liberation theology in order to create a broad external framework
in which to house the internal subjective voice.

In my work with these Black young people, I was anxious
that their reflections and comments regarding truth-telling
and integrity should be placed within a broader context.
What were the factors that influenced their notions of truth-
telling? When is it inappropriate to 'tell the whole truth, so
help me God'? Beckford, in his theological reflections on
gang violence in Britain, challenges the urban church to
engage in this internal and external form of analysis.[44]

So, to sum up, this particular approach to undertaking
Black theology is one that seeks to use creative interdisciplinary models for theological reflection, which is now common
parlance within the broader arena of 'practical theology',[45]
alongside the penetrating analysis and searing insights of constructive and systematic theology. This approach to undertaking Black theology is one that is attempting to breach
the gap between the academy and the Church, between

grassroots believers and academics. It is a commitment to using the experiences and the agency of ordinary Black people as raw materials for an interactive approach to constructive theology using the techniques and methods from practical theology. In effect, an interactive methodology for doing Black theology.

2. The Role of Black Theology within Secular and Plural Contexts

CAROL TROUPE

This chapter examines the issues surrounding the development of a religious education resource that incorporates the experiences, cultures and histories of Black communities into teaching about Christianity in schools. It looks not only at the concerns of bringing Black theology into a new environment, but at the contribution it can make to the education of young people in this context.

My focus on Black theology's possible role beyond the Church originates from my research, which looked at using an approach to school religious education influenced by this theological standpoint.[1] Here, I look at some of the issues raised by placing Black theology into a context of ethnic and religious plurality, where educational rather than theological concerns are paramount. In terms of how this fits in with ideas of ministry, I have taken my understanding of this beyond the confines of the Church. If ministry is understood as encompassing ideas about the work of God in the world, I would say that attempting to take Black theology into a new context offers new possibilities for this work to take place.

Why bring Black theology into the new context?

The motivation for taking Black theology into a new, non-church environment grew out of exploring how Black Christian experience was being approached within religious education. Eric Pemberton, both in his MPhil thesis[2] and in his various roles within education, has emphasized the need to include the breadth of Caribbean and African religious experience in school curricula.[3] Taking a different approach, the resource pack produced by Becher[4] provided insights into the histories, practices and beliefs of Black-led churches. As well as work such as this, there have been attempts to include Black Christian and more generally Black religious experience in the agreed syllabuses of several local authorities.[5]

It was not my intention to repeat the work that had already been done but rather to approach the subject in a new and different way. Was there a way to explore Christianity from a Black perspective within religious education without focusing on particular churches, doctrines or practices? It appeared to me that Black theology provided a way to do this but that transferring it to a new context could have implications.

The claims and aims of Black theology

When Cone wrote about Black theology in the late 1960s and early 1970s, he was very clear about his intentions: '. . . there is, then, a desperate need for a black theology, a theology whose sole purpose is to apply the freeing power of the gospel to black people under white oppression'.[6] This was a theology that developed as a response to an ongoing history of racism and oppression, where the White Church was content to proclaim the gospel while still denying the humanity of Black people. While it is true that Black communities were already well-practised in reinterpreting Christianity in light of their experience, Black theology went a step further and made strong claims about the focus of God's interest and what God desired for the world: 'God is not color-blind in the black–white struggle, but has made an unqualified identification with blacks. This means that the movement for black liberation is the very work of God, effecting God's will among men.'[7] The focus on ideas of God's identification with Black people and the 'Blackness' of Jesus himself are an attempt to provide Black communities with a means of not only seeing the important connections between the Scripture and their own experiences, but also as validation of their humanity, and motivation and justification for working towards their own liberation. As Hopkins states, 'Black Theology, therefore, is an effort of African American people to claim their blackness and their freedom as people of God.'[8]

Within a Black Christian environment, even if some might see these claims around the privileging of 'Blackness' as contentious, their value is evident. In a context where a theology perceived by most as universal[9] had at worst been used to oppress and deny Black humanity and at best had failed to challenge oppression and racism, this theological exploration from a Black perspective was essential. However, in what way could it manifest itself beyond this context and what role, if any, could it play there?

In my attempt to take Black theology into religious education aimed at Key Stage 2 and Lower Key Stage 3,[10] there were two main concerns to be considered. The first of these being that there would be no room to explain the complex issues behind the development and claims of Black theology and therefore it would be easier not to state them explicitly.[11] The second issue was that it was likely that the groups using the material in this environment would be neither exclusively Black nor entirely Christian nor even religious. In answer to the first point, my concern was that by not stating or emphasizing the claims of Black theology, could this really be described as a Black theology-influenced approach to religious education? In terms of the second issue, was there any value in attempting to utilize Black theology in a context for which it was never intended?

A wider interpretation of Black theology

In order to address these concerns, it was necessary to move beyond Cone's original work into a wider understanding of what Black theology could encompass. It is the exploration of the group of thinkers within Black theology that Frederick Ware describes as the Black Philosophical School[12] that enables a very challenging examination and critique of Black theology.[13] It is not my intention here to enter into an extensive discussion of their ideas but rather to explain briefly how these ideas enabled me to see how my work could be situated within Black theology. My concerns centred on the fact that while it was inappropriate in the context in which I was working to make explicit statements about Black people and their liberation being divinely favoured, or about Jesus being Black (literally or symbolically) would these omissions place my work outside the limits of Black theology? Furthermore, what would an approach to religious education focused on Black communities offer to a more plural, educational context.

The work of those within the Black Philosophical School does not totally reject ideas of liberation or the focus on Black faith, culture or experience. The difference comes from the interpretations of what constitutes liberation and also the justifications for pursuing that liberation, using humanist frameworks as well as (not exclusively Christian) theistic ones. For this group, liberation is not limited to or justified by either the Bible or Black experience. 'Liberation is defined using social and political philosophies that may or may not be compatible, at all points, with the Bible or black story.'[14]

Here, liberation is to be valued because it is something that human beings desire, not because God desires it for them.[15] The issue of using Black cultures, histories and experiences as prime sources of study does not depend on a perceived divine favour. Within this framework, Black lives are worthy in and of themselves as a valid part of humanity. Ware describes how '[t]he humanist tradition, as West understands it, has no need to sacralize blackness in order to legitimate the study of African American life and culture'.[16]

This is not to say that the religious education material I eventually produced entirely embraced the Black Philosophical School approach and rejected the ideas of Cone and his colleagues. My work, though placed in a plural, non-confessional context, still had to focus on Christianity and it was my intention to retain the use of Black cultures, stories and experiences as my framework. However, this exploration allowed the possibility that Black theology did not have to be confined by particular tenets or limited to use in entirely Black religious contexts and highlighted the critique and development that had been taking place within the discipline since the early work of Cone.

Black theology's contribution to the education of young people

As I stated earlier, my second concern centred on the role Black theology could play once it was moved out of a Black Christian context into one that was not only religiously and ethnically plural, but also non-confessional. Within this environment, it was my belief that, more than just allowing an exploration of Black Christianity, Black theology had a particular contribution to make to education. Here, I use the word not to describe the amassing of facts and figures in order to pass examinations, but rather refer to what Naidoo describes as 'real education as opposed to convenient training'.[17]

It is my belief that this contribution falls into several categories. The first of these is that it allows Black Christian experience to be explored in a way that does not depend on descriptions of particular denominations or practices; this approach is very much concerned with how, for example, God is perceived and what faith can mean to adherents within particular contexts. The contribution this particular point makes to the education of young people is that, in terms of looking at Christianity within religious education, it provides a framework within which pupils can move beyond simply looking at the outward trappings of particular faiths. For example, looking at Easter moves beyond descriptions of how Easter is celebrated in different churches or exploring issues of life after death.[18] Within a Black theology framework, Easter becomes symbolic of Jesus' solidarity with oppressed peoples and the belief in the possibility of their liberation, spiritual and otherwise. Through the influence of Black theology in a religious education context, pupils are given the opportunity to explore aspects of faith from a completely different perspective and also to recognize how the histories, cultures and environments of faith adherents lead to a diversity of belief and understanding *within* as well as between religions and denominations; a diversity that does not manifest itself simply through differences in worship practices.

The second point I would make about Black theology's contribution to education is partly linked to this first point; in that it allows pupils to explore the more *practical* aspects of the Christian faith. Since Black theology was born out of the oppressed and marginalized situations in which Black people found themselves and is very much focused on issues surrounding those situations such as justice, liberation and equality, it facilitates a study of Christianity that is largely concerned with these very issues. This is not to say that the spiritual aspect is ignored but that there is a definite sense of the need to effect change. This social justice aspect of Black theology is useful to the education of young people, as it provides, through its very nature, a framework within which to think more critically about how the world operates and ask questions about fairness and equality.

The 'Bellyful' exercise from the Cream Project resource is an example of this,[19] as it brings to light, through a group activity, instances of inequality and injustice that exist in the world. In a context such as this, Christian action becomes more than 'being nice' or 'do-gooding' but rather is grounded in a sense of justice and concerns about how to effect that justice. This is also helpful on another issue; the perception of Christianity among young people. A Black theology approach enables young people to understand that

Christian belief is not necessarily as disempowering as they may perceive it to be; I feel that this can be especially important in the case of young Black people who may see Christianity as something that has 'enslaved' Black communities, stripped them of their identity, and made them subservient and passive.

Black theology provides an illustration of how Black communities need not compromise their cultures or forget their histories in order to embrace Christianity, but can actually interpret and express their faith through those elements. It also provides a means by which to illustrate how Black people have actually been *empowered* by their Christianity, and have used it as motivation for action towards their *own* liberation. Black theology provides a framework within which to explore ways in which Black communities have been mobilized into responding to situations of injustice and oppression and defied limitations placed upon them by society throughout history.

This leads me to my third point; the important position of Black history, experience and culture within Black theology. This is well-illustrated within the work of Anthony Reddie in *Growing into Hope* and is largely retained on the Cream Project; here not only is the work based on the precepts of Black theology but also, the various cultural products of Black communities are used as ways of learning about Christianity. The material uses stories, plays and sketches, illustrations, quizzes and real-life personalities inspired by and drawn from Black communities as part of the teaching process.

In this way, the cultures and experiences of Black pupils can be highlighted and affirmed and at the same time, a way is provided for *all* pupils to become more informed about histories and cultures within the African diaspora, while remaining within a religious education context. For example, in the lesson entitled 'Variety of Gifts'[20] on the Cream Project, pupils not only learn about the concept of the Church as the body of Christ, but about food from the

Caribbean and Africa and through this are introduced to ideas about the interconnectedness of different countries and issues of fair trading. In the 'Journeys and Expectations'[21] section, as well as looking at the traditional story of Jesus' entry into Jerusalem, pupils are encouraged to take part in a Black general knowledge quiz and also learn about post-war migration from the Caribbean. Thus, Black theology emphasizes the value and facilitates the exploration of Black histories and cultures within a religious education setting, encouraging the cross-curricular learning that is often sought by educators. The use of historical figures and events within Black communities may also assist in the widening of pupils' knowledge in the area of History as a curriculum subject.

This takes me to my final point; Black theology, while based in religious education, facilitates learning that feeds into other subject areas. The link with the area of SMSC[22] is obvious, since this is often explicitly associated with religious education; however, the underlying concerns of Black theology add a further dimension to the contribution religious education can make. The contribution to cultural development is perhaps the most obvious, since the use of Black historical and cultural sources that is central to this theology encourages engagement with issues around culture that go beyond religious practice. For pupils who share that culture, it can offer affirmation and empowerment, for those outside that experience (and also those within it) there is the opportunity for learning and exploration.

The contribution to spiritual development can almost be taken for granted in a religious education environment and perhaps it is here that Black young people might find opportunity for the most benefit from religious education underpinned by Black theology (this is not to say that there are not benefits to be had for other pupils). The guidelines for SMSC on the National Curriculum website state: 'Pupils' spiritual development involves the growth of their sense of self, their unique potential, their understanding of their strengths and weaknesses, and their will to achieve.'[23] Black theology provides Black pupils with an opportunity to explore these issues within religious education in a way which may speak directly to them through their identification with aspects of the histories and communities that are being explored.

In terms of social and moral development, again through its connections with matters of justice, freedom and equality, and the focus on community as well as individual struggle and empowerment, Black theology provides opportunities to consider issues such as right and wrong, decision-making, community responsibility and what it means to belong.[24]

A religious education that incorporates aspects of Black theology may also contribute to areas of PSHE (personal, social and health education) and citizenship, allowing students to look critically at the way the world operates and at questions of social justice, emphasizing Black cultural elements. This contributes to topics such as 'preparing to play an active role as citizens' and 'developing good relationships and respecting the differences between people'[25] and for older pupils, 'knowledge and understanding about becoming informed citizens' and 'developing skills of enquiry and communication'.[26]

Thus far, I have discussed how Black theology can make a particular contribution to religious education, while also feeding into other areas of the curriculum. As well as providing a means to explore Black Christian experience in an alternative way and incorporating elements of Black histories and cultures into the curriculum, it encourages an awareness of social issues at even the most basic level. This provides opportunities for pupils to explore a much wider understanding of what faith is and how it plays out in the lives of adherents and in society as a whole. It could also be used in a similar way with older age groups but here one could take it further by actually discussing and debating the theological ideas at its origin. However, having offered ideas for the role of Black theology in an educational setting, there are still issues that need to be addressed.

Further considerations

Two concerns remain in terms of taking Black theology into this new context. In order to facilitate the move into a non-confessional, plural environment, could the Black theology presented there be seen as 'watered down' or unrepresentative?[27] My second concern centres on the emphasis I have placed on the social justice elements of liberation in this context. This tends to minimize the importance of the spiritual aspects of liberation that would be present within a religious environment, and perhaps neglects the exploration of an important aspect of Black faith experience. I feel that conveying the significance of this spiritual element accurately would be difficult and could perhaps only be achieved by direct interaction and dialogue between religious education pupils and members of faith communities.

3. Black British Theology in Gospel Music

DULCIE A. DIXON MCKENZIE

Introduction

Since its advent in the early 1950s, Black British gospel music has outgrown its incubatory locality within the Black Church, and unwittingly advanced into wider British society.[1] It has evolved into a public musical art form, and gratuitously matured into a commercial commodity that is consumed in circumstances far removed from its original creation and purpose.[2]

A most disturbing truth, however, is that the proliferation of Black British gospel music is a phenomenon that has been neglected by scholars, notably Black British theologians. It has progressed without formal systematic theological assessment, and a direct result of its exclusion is a noticeable absence of theological commentary on Black British gospel music, and its contribution to both Black Christianity and British society.

In sum, with one exception,[3] Black British gospel music is insignificant in Black British theological discourse. Essentially, academics have ignored the social, political, cultural, historical, educational and geographical concerns of Black British gospel music, particularly the strategies employed for its survival, to 'sing the Lord's song in this strange land' (Psalm 137.4). In many ways, the land is still strange, without an insiders' historical scholastic narrative of the origin and expedition of Black British gospel music.

So far the identity of Black British gospel music is subsumed in the historical narrative of African-American gospel music, and there is very little awareness or appreciation of its uniqueness, particularly the narrative of its originality and the traditions that have shaped its evolution in British society. In stating this, I want to point to the extent to which Black British gospel music carries a postcolonial identity that not only draws from African-American sources, but of equal importance, from African and Caribbean roots with which one has to engage and consider.

Regrettably, the history of Black British gospel music is a 'lost story' and as a direct result, there is no historical or theological understanding of its pilgrimage so far. The voyage of Black British gospel music is what Kortright Davis describes as a continuing experience of Egypt: 'If you do not know your Egypt, you cannot know your Exodus.'[4]

Until there is an insider's scholarly study tracing the history of Black British gospel music, there will continue to be a distorted understanding of its history. In the meantime, inherent in the theological qualities of Black British gospel music, is a crisis of identity. To be specific, there is a collision between roots and routes, which Black British theologian Robert Beckford examines in his groundbreaking work *Jesus Is Dread: Black Theology and Black Culture in Britain*. Beckford reflects on the symbols, icons and systems within both the Black church tradition and Black British expressive culture, calling for new ways of engaging in theological discourse in Black communities.

In line with Beckford's thesis is the question of Black liturgies entering mainstream White churches through the back door. For instance, the appropriation and exploitation of Black church music has been a longstanding state of affairs, where the music and influence of Black British gospel music is utilized without significant recognition.

Beckford correctly identifies White gospel songwriter Graham Kendrick as a perpetrator. Kendrick employs a prominent musician from the Black church tradition, as his musical director. Steve Thompson is a prolific pianist, raised within the Black church tradition as the son of a Black Pentecostal minister. He became established within the New Testament Church of God, beginning with the Majestic Singers (a choir based in Birmingham), before working with numerous choirs and groups in Britain and overseas.

Kendrick extends his exploitation of Black British gospel music to singers, whereby he 'uses' those who are highly regarded within the Black church tradition and the Black British gospel music circuit, for example, Delroy Hutchinson, Godfrey Gayle and Tracey Riggan. This appears to be a growing trend within White Christian music, with artists such as Matt Redman, Chris Bowater, who also use established Black musicians and singers such as Noel Robinson, Mark Beswick, Paul Lee and Carla Hayles and others, to 'advance' their music. Of course, it must be stated that these Black artists who are being 'used' do so with a degree of complicity, choosing to make advantage of such opportunities in order to further their careers.

It can be argued, however, that in a similar way, Black British gospel music is guilty of appropriating other sources and influences without recognition, while adopting 'alien' influences, thereby decontextualizing their own experience. In this regard, Black British gospel is not unlike all cultural forms of production in its borrowing and synthesizing of disparate sources, themes and modes of thinking in the furthering of its own development. For instance, the influence of African-American gospel music is evident in Black British gospel music. In many ways, Black British gospel artists have adopted the musical language and mannerisms of African-American gospel music. This adaptation has been undertaken without due regard for the postcolonial artistic legacy of their own African-Caribbean roots and influences.

To demonstrate this apparent disregard of their heritage, I point to an interesting situation which occurred in 2001. An African-American gospel music singer, Donnie McClurkin, came to Britain to record one of his albums. The finished product featured a 'Caribbean Medley', which was a collaboration of Caribbean choruses that are familiar, but unfortunately, made redundant within the predominantly Pentecostal church tradition in Britain.[5] On the album Donnie McClurkin attempts to introduce the medley in Jamaican patois, and encourages the audience (who were Black British) 'to be true to themselves and help him sing the song'.

In this situation, we have an African-American gospel artist, endorsing 'Caribbeanism' in gospel music. The irony of this performance is that since its release, the actual choruses within Donnie McClurkin's Caribbean medley have been reintroduced into the liturgy of the modern Black church tradition. In effect, it has taken an African-American to reintroduce an important element of the African-Caribbean religio-cultural heritage back into the liturgical practices of predominantly Pentecostal church practice in Britain. As a direct result of this recording, Black British gospel artists and the younger members of the congregation, now proudly sing, 'I've Got my Mind Made up', 'Born, Born, Born Again, Thank God I'm Born Again', 'Fire, Fire Fire, Fire Fall on Me', etc.

My contention is that Black British gospel music artists have detached themselves from their diasporan and postcolonial roots, in favour of an African-American religio-cultural tradition. To be specific, they have separated themselves from their historical roots, and as a result, their lyrical content and prophetic role seriously lacks a 'gospel' message from a Black British worldview. Their lyrical content is not a portrayal of their own language and vocabulary; neither does it articulate Black Christianity in Britain.[6] Instead, Black British gospel music adopts and misappropriates African-American ideology in their attempt to 'cross over' into wider British society. At the time of writing, I am unable to detail the specifics of these developments, but in future work I will examine the lyrical content of some of the prolific Black British gospel artists in Britain, such as 'Raymond and Co', 'Siani', 'Nu Life' and 'GK Real'.

For decades, within predominantly Black Pentecostalism,

there has been a tendency to imitate populist White evangeli-cal churches.[7] As well as the liturgy, they have also borrowed the songs and shaped them to fit their need.[8] For instance, during the eighteenth and nineteenth century, White evangel-ists wrote many of the favourite songs that have a fixed place in Black hymnody. For example, D. L. Moody, Ira D. Sankey, Fanny J.Crosby, and Robert Lowry wrote such songs as: 'Blessed Assurance Jesus is mine', 'A Shelter in the Time of Storm', 'I am Thine oh Lord', 'Jesus Keep Me Near the Cross', 'We're Marching to Zion', etc. Again, in my future work, I intend to select and examine some of these songs in an attempt to explicate the influence of Euro-American hymnody on the worship of Black Pentecostalism in Britain.

I will anchor my argument in the theological sensibilities of the first generation of Caribbean worshippers, who through their experience of racism and oppression as new arrivals in this British society, demonstrated a 'lived theology' in their music. Their songs were a critique of their societal situation, and tackled the themes that were a part of Black oppression.

By contrast, the lyrical content of contemporary Black British gospel music does not reflect an obvious or overly accurate picture of history or present experience. Instead, there is greater emphasis on structure rather than substance. In effect, there is little of significant theological import in contemporary Black British gospel music. It is in danger of separating itself from its original purpose of worship, and of losing its prophetic role in Black Christianity and British society.

This research is in the process of detailing the 'identity crisis' in Black British gospel music. I believe that it is uncriti-cally African-Americanized, which is evident in the lyrical content, musical form and language and more critically, its historical account of originality. This essay is part of a longer ongoing piece of research that is seeking to make the case for the importance of Black British theology in Black British gospel music, in order to preserve its African-Caribbean roots and to provide a theological meaning for life.

4. The Letter Kills but the Spirit Gives Life

BERESFORD LEWIS

Introduction

The title of this paper, a quotation from 2 Corinthians 3.6, represents a disjunction between what is outwardly professed and the inner meaning of a life in the Spirit. This is characterized by the difference between orthodoxy and orthopraxis. Orthodoxy is thinking or believing the right thing in contrast to orthopraxis, which is concerned with doing the right thing. The issue is not what people say in doctrinal statements or Christian dogmas but rather what people do in reality. There is, it seems, a need to bring belief and practice into alignment – hence the tension between orthodoxy and orthopraxis. On the one hand, the pursuit of the inner meaning is for salvation. On the other, what is outwardly professed seems to be in opposition to the works of the Holy Spirit as the agency for transformation. The title of this paper represents an unhealthy and unresolved tension between the professed and the inner meaning in the pursuit of the life in the Spirit.

In her PhD thesis entitled '"Breaking Every Fetter": To What Extent Has the Black-led Church in Britain Developed a Theology of Liberation?' Valentina Alexander argued in 1996 that African-Caribbean Churches in Britain 'appeared to pursue a vigorous and implicit radicalism while verbalizing and protecting the ethos of a conservative value system'.[1] This quotation represents what Alexander calls 'the two faces' of African-Caribbean Christianity. The first is the public face, or what is outwardly professed, which appears to be passive, and conservative. It is also restricting, limiting and controlling because of its imperialist, colonialist and now neo-colonial attitudes. The task of the Church, however, is not to protect the status quo but to transform it. In this context, James Harris in his book *Pastoral Theology* argues: '[t]he church is called to deal with moral questions so that it and society will be transformed, not in order to fit into the prevailing social and political milieu'.[2] This takes us on to Alexander's second point, which she calls the private face of the Church. It is a search for a life in the Spirit, which is rooted in the concrete struggle for liberation. Here liberation means 'freedom from want, the concrete substance of all freedom'[3] and a struggle to realize one's full human potential. This is the face that is seeking fulfilment in the works of the Holy Spirit and represents a grassroots struggle, a struggle from the bottom up, for a fuller and more holistic life, based on the liberating works of the Holy Spirit. These two faces of African-Caribbean Christianity symbolize a series of tensions, which are cultural, theological, economical and political. These tensions manifest themselves at local, national and international levels.

In this chapter I am using Alexander's research findings as a basis to argue that the conflict between the public and private faces of African-Caribbean churches in Britain serves to frustrate rather than help them to carry out their prophetic role leading to salvation. In this paper I want to explore two important themes in relation to those tensions. The first is the issue of inculturation and the second is the scholar/practitioner divide. Both of these areas, I will argue, have the potential to act as vehicles for bridging the gap between the public and private faces of African-Caribbean churches in Britain.

This chapter will employ the concepts of (1) celebration, (2) dialogical relationships and (3) critical and constructive criticism as (a) a method and (b) a methodology for bridging the gap between 'those who sit in the pews, preach in pulpits and teach in seminaries'.[4] By 'method' I mean the techniques or procedures used in gathering and analysing data relating to a question or hypothesis, whereas 'methodology' is used to mean the analysis of how research is done or should proceed.[5] Next I will explain how the two themes will be used but first some terminological clarifications.

Culture

I see culture as a vehicle for shaping and organizing the collective consciousness of a people representing their complete way of life. As Chrisman writes: 'Culture is a vehicle for developing, shaping and organising a people and their consciousness, representing their collective values, aesthetics, ethics and laws as well as their spiritual directions.'[6]

Inculturation

Inculturation is concerned with the complex web of interactions between the gospel and different cultures. These are interactions where emphasis constantly shifts, where nuances change, where things are forgotten and where new insights are constructed.[7] Inculturation as it is used here means the way people respond to the gospel message from their own self-understanding from within their own unique cultural and historical context.

British Black theology

'Theology', Lartey asserts 'is what is articulated about God.' 'Black theology', then, 'refers to what is said, believed and expressed through various media by Black people concerning God.'[8] In this general sense Black theology 'is concerned with the experience of black people everywhere'.[9] However, British 'Black theology . . . is seeking to make known what Black people in Britain are thinking, feeling, saying and expressing about their experience of God.'[10] Furthermore, British Black theology is a critique of Western Christian theologies[11] as well as 'a response to a white theology which sanctifies racist social institutions'.[12] Lartey, taking a contextual approach, maintains that 'black[s] in Britain have their own peculiar character'[13] pointing out that Black theology emerged within an · American and South African context and although lessons can be learnt from other contexts, he believes that Blacks in Britain should develop their own brand of Black theology which reflects their own realities.

Accordingly, Lartey suggests 'we must look carefully at the British experience if we are to develop a useful theology'.[14] Being conscious of the wider debate on Black theology on both sides of the Atlantic or what Paul Gilroy calls the Black Atlantic, I shall make a particular effort where possible to engage with the Black theological discourse in Britain, especially the work produced by the *Black Theology: An International Journal*, as noted already. However, as the title of Roswith Gerloff's seminal two volumes *A Plea for Black British Theologies* suggests, there is no single British Black theology. But this is obscured by the signifier 'Black' which is used to describe different social groups. It is therefore necessary to stipulate further how the term 'Black' is used in relation to British Black theologies.

Black as a signifier: the search for existence and then essence

The signifier 'Black' as in Black theology, Black majority churches (BMCs) or Black-led churches is often used as an umbrella term within a political context to describe a wide range of different social groups of people from Africa, the Caribbean and Asia or non-white people from former colonial and commonwealth countries and their descendents.[15] Even so, this categorization marks social groups, which are culturally, linguistically, historically, politically and religiously different. Therefore, Black as a signifier is imprecise and problematic since no such homogeneous category exists.[16]

According to Lartey, politically, anyone could be described as 'Black' if they 'identify with "the Black experience" in terms of heritage, oppression and domination'.[17] This view is in alignment with Cone's notion of ontological or symbolic Blackness where the signifier Black has nothing to do with skin colour but rather the identification with those who are oppressed and suffering.[18] By altering the definition of Blackness, Cone has provided a basis for breaking away from certain forms of social control and establishing new forms of being. On this matter, Gergen observes '[to] alter description and explanation is thus to threaten certain actions and to invite others'.[19] So in altering the description of Black and providing a different explanation, Cone shows that the signifier Black is void of essentialist qualities and therefore has no fixed meaning, although essentialist thinkers would disagree with this. Similarly, Christian describes 'black as persons/groups who can claim African heritage throughout the world'.[20] In fact all persons or groups can fit Christian's description based on the view that African is 'the cradle of the human race'.[21] So it can be seen that without clarification the signifier Black can be confusing.

Both Jagessar[22] and Pityana[23] see the Caribbean and its diaspora churches as culturally plural. In this context, one can talk about an African, East Indian, White and Chinese Caribbean, which are reflected here in Britain.[24] Hence there is a need for a more inclusive language when discussing British Black theologies and BMCs.

Sturge uses the term BMCs to mean 'churches emerging from the African and Caribbean diaspora'.[25] The *Black Community Report* calls for more precision on how the signifier Black is used, therefore, wherever the terms Black-led, Black Majority Churches or African-Caribbean Christ-ianity, except where stated otherwise, refer mainly to, but not exclusively to churches emerging from the English speak-ing Caribbean and represents people of African-Caribbean descent.[26] An attempt has been made here not to conflate different social groups under a Black banner. While this means that some people who might otherwise have been included are now excluded, it does make it possible to focus on the specific needs of a particular community. Having attempted to clarify some of the key terms used in this chapter, I will proceed with the discussion on inculturation in the section that follows.

Crises and more crises

The concept of inculturation is used to explore the relationship between different cultures and the gospel and how this in turn impacts on evangelism, which is about 'proclaiming Christ in word and deed', and mission, which is 'the total activity of the church as it reaches out into the world'.[27] The link between the gospel and culture is stressed in the works of Robert Beckford, Anthony Reddie, Ronald Nathan and others. However, in attempting to address the issue of inculturation I want in particular to focus on Nathan's Pan-African theology because he seems to offer a more comprehensive programme for dealing with the issue of inculturation.

There are a series of major crises facing BMCs and the African-Caribbean Community in Britain. Some researchers have explained these crises in terms of socio-political, socio-economic and theological concerns. Others tend to focus on culture and identity but all those concerns overlap in interesting and complex ways.[28] Marcia Dixon proclaims '[t]he black community is currently experiencing a crisis with its youth'.[29] Likewise Joe Aldred[30] goes further in stating that BMCs in Britain are not only facing a youth crisis but also churches are facing stagnation and to some degrees irrelevance.

These are not only concerns for the Pentecostal and Charismatic churches but also for the so-called mainstream churches.[31] Moltmann in his book *The Crucified God* identifies what he calls a 'double crisis' in Christianity – 'the *crisis of relevance* and the *crisis of identity*' (italics in the original).[32] According to Moltmann '[t]his double crisis can be more accurately described as the *identity-involvement dilemma*'.[33] So the crises identified within BMCs are not new but a reflection of global crises of relevance and identity within Christianity, as Moltmann points out.

I have been attending the Black Theology Forum in Birmingham since I embarked on a PhD programme which attempts to establish how and in what ways BMCs are responding to the plight of the African-Caribbean community at local, regional and national levels in Britain. I have also attended a number of BMC conferences, conventions and meetings. What is noticeable is that the Black theologians appear to be absent from such meetings. During some of the discussions at the Forum in Birmingham, a question, which is often raised, concerns the relationship between those doing Black theology and BMCs. Some suggested that there was too wide a margin between the two and that there is an urgent need to bridge the gap.

Additionally, I noticed that in 2003 the New Testament Church of God (NTCOG) started a programme called The Big Move an acronym which stands for (1) Building committed confident leaders (2) Informing and impacting our youth (3) Growing healthy churches (4) Mobilizing the church for ministry and mission (5) Offering hope and leadership to our community (6) Valuing our women and men (7) Evangelizing our communities.[34] I was particularly interested to find out whether items (2), informing and impacting our youth, and (4), mobilizing the church for ministry and mission, would benefit from the research conducted by those doing British Black theology. So it was from this angle that I thought to scrutinize the work of *Black Theology: An International Journal* more closely, especially on the themes of inculturation, evangelism and mission. This led me to raise questions about the role of British Black theologies in impacting on BMCs and how issues affecting those churches were reflected upon in the *Journal*.

The *Journal* proclaims its mission as providing educational resources in the fields of theology, culture and religion as well as providing a critique of BMCs and the Black community (Africans, African-Caribbeans and Asians). So I was keen to find out what kind of dialogue was taking place between British Black theologians and BMCs, especially in the light of comments made by Beckford who argues that the relationship is problematic. Also the issue of inculturation seems to stand out in a highly significant way. Aldred appears to highlight this when he writes:

> Black people of every generation and of every location know, either by instinct or by experience, the repercussions of White missionary activities that for centuries have ridden roughshod over Black cultural heritage in their quest to establish their version of the truth of the gospel of Jesus Christ.[35]

Aldred's observation made four years ago, now suggests that the time may be right to engage in such a debate, looking specifically at its impact on BMCs in multicultural Britain.

Culture, Evangelism, Mission and Inculturation

The structure and design of The Big Move at different levels brings into sharp focus the issue of evangelism and missions but more than that, it is as much about culture and identity issues, crucial for all BMCs in Britain. Culture is important for evangelism and mission. This is given voice by Anderson[36] when he stresses the need to understand how cultural changes affect BMCs, families and communities. Similarly, Simmonds writes, 'Black worship [is] somehow conditioned by black imagery of God and the relational concepts of these imageries must meet the cultural needs of people.'[37] Additionally, Mohabir observes that '[c]ulture is linked with people's, past, present and future, carried as a baggage by a group, family and society'.[38] A view that is often put forward is that BMCs are still influenced by enslavement, colonialism and neo-colonialism and need to set themselves free from such entrenched ideologies.[39] Evangelism, culture and mission appear to be heading for a dangerous collision and a battle for cultural supremacy in multicultural Britain.

At the heart of the inculturation debate is the significance of and the role of culture in the propagation of the gospel. The question is what role culture should play and whether the Christian message can be authenticated without destroying the cultural heritage of people receiving the gospel. Williams[40] raises some serious questions about the relationship between the gospel and culture by asking: What has God to do with the origins of cultures? How, for example, should the gospel be understood in the light of culture? Which culture? And whose culture? These are crucial questions many BMCs are asking.

The question of how cultures and the gospel should interact raises other concerns about cultural dominance and power/knowledge relationships and the effects of enslavement, imperialism and colonialism, which have been influential in mission and evangelism in the last five hundred years in Africa, the Caribbean and other parts of the world. The term 'inculturation' is problematic because different people use it to mean different things. Schreiter[41] for example, gets directly to the point by asking the all-important question, whether Christians should start with faith or culture.

As a way of propagating the gospel, inculturation is necessary because 'faith cannot take root' without culture. Inculturation is also important because it provides 'the possibility of new and deeper insights into the meaning of the mystery of Christ'.[42] Williams quotes Payne who recognizes the universality of Christ in all culture. Importantly, this opens the door for others to co-opt Christ into their own culture without being subordinated to any other culture. Therefore Christ has to be Asianized, Africanized or African-Caribbeanized in order to become a truly universal Christ – a Christ of the world, a Christ for everyone within his or her own cultural and historical context. Payne sees this as a problem. He writes:

[W]e [non-Europeans] must not complain that the Europeans 'Europeanized' Christ. Christ had to become a
European in order to deliver Europeans from evil. This
helps to understand why, when the Europeans shared
Christ with us, it was a European Christ that they shared.[43]

Many African-Caribbean youths are turning away from the
Church because as Coleman suggests, the Europeanized Christ
is the dominant image that they are presented with and not a
Christ who is part of their own culture. Coleman notes: 'The
gospel itself . . . has become so closely identified with
Westernism and imperialism that one of the most common
objections to be heard from black youth today is that it is a
"white man's religion".'[44] Coleman's response to this argument is that it is far from the truth. However, she admits
that it is a sad reality because such 'sentiment is actively and
passively being reinforced at many levels in our churches'.[45]
According to Nathan: 'For many Black youths the Black
churches' message of redemption without emancipation
from mental slavery is unacceptable. Its equation of holiness
with cultural abandonment in favour of Eurocentric systems,
celebrations and norms is unacceptable.'[46] Nathan therefore
offers a Pan-African theology, which is Afrocentric in nature,
a theology that affirms African values as a way of helping to
resolve the issue of inculturation. He draws on sources from
Black theology, Caribbean theology and African theology in
order to construct four distinctive features of a Pan-African
theology.

First, Nathan stresses the notion of harmony 'between all
created order, that is, the Supreme Being (Creator), divinities, ancestors and the environment'.[47] Second, he maintains
that a Pan-African theology is holistic in which dualism does
not exist and where the sacred and the secular, the material
and the spiritual are assumed to co-exist. Third, a Pan-
African theology is an experiential theology, which 'starts
with the situation of the local context and the local people'.[48]
Finally, a Pan-African theology is action oriented addressing

itself to the concrete concerns of those on the margin and those who are hurting. Even if Nathan admits that this is just one way of doing theology, what is interesting about Nathan's Pan-African theology is that he makes it into a programme for liberation.

Liberation churches

When BMCs become liberating churches the following would be possible according to Nathan. First, they 'would have to develop liberation-centred theological institutions that produce Christian leaders who understand their mission to include community development and community leadership'.[49] Second, they 'would celebrate their blackness without apology for their African heritage. This would be reflected in their symbols, literature, architecture, theology, hymnology, music, worship and dance.'[50] Nathan maintains that liberating churches 'would resist cultural assimilation and integration and seek out ways of promoting diversity'. The central focus of mission and evangelization would be liberating people from social injustice, unemployment, poverty, etc. Finally, liberating churches 'will tackle corruption in local and central government as well as in ecclesiastical circles'. Being a liberating church in no way threatens the spirituality of BMCs 'but would tap into the gifts of all their members which in turn would stimulate growth' and transformation.[51]

Having focused on the issue of inculturation in the first part of this chapter, in the second part I will consider the function of British Black theologies in helping to empower the local churches and their leaders.

Bridging the gap: addressing the scholar–practitioner divide

Beckford asked 'Can [British] Black Theology become a viable theology for Black Majority Churches?'[52] In the acknowledgements to his first book, *Jesus Is Dread*, Beckford was keen to attempt to 'stimulate discussion and critical dialogue between those who sit in the pews, preach from the pulpit and teach in seminaries'.[53] Four years later he appears to doubt whether British Black theology can become a viable theology for BMCs in Britain. Beckford's question at the beginning of this paragraph seems to highlight a tension between BMCs and those doing British Black theology. Beckford offers three reasons why he thinks the intersection among those who sit in pews, preach in pulpits and teach in seminaries is problematic and an uphill battle. Beckford is partly wrong in his first two reasons and although his third point is a generally accepted position among many researchers on BMCs, he does not appear to reflect important and ongoing shifts in the theory of the Holy Spirit – pneumatology.

In this section I will briefly outline the reasons Beckford gives for arguing that British Black theology is not a viable theology for BMCs. Finally I want to offer celebration, dialogical relationships and critical and constructive criticism as a methodology and a way of bridging the gap among those who sit in pews, preach in pulpits and teach in seminaries.

The battle: uniting hearts and minds

Beckford's first argument is the position that, 'Black Majority congregations are still terrified of discussing anything seemingly political from the pulpit'.[54] This position has been changing for a long time and there seems to be ample evidence to suggest that BMCs are using the pulpit to discuss political issues. But Beckford seems reluctant to document such stories. The classic text on this issue is a recent book edited by Joe Aldred.[55] This work is a collection of 20 sermons by Black preachers representing different Christian denominations in Britain covering a wide range of socio-political concerns. Already in 2000, making reference to this book, Beckford states, '[s]ome Black preachers are beginning to take seriously multi-dimensional analysis of the text'.[56] Yet, Beckford makes no mention of the fact that the book was dealing with socio-political issues from the pulpit.

It is, however, not clear what Beckford means by political. Here politics is 'the art and process of gaining, maintaining and using power'. Where power is 'the social capacity of a group to realise its will even in opposition to others' and the social (structural) capacity of a group represents the 'organizational and institutional ability of the group to realize its will – even in opposition to others'.[57] Aldred's most likely conclusion to the sermons is that 'writers are dealing with a range of issues that affect or interest them'.[58] According to one interviewer cited in Alexander '[t]here's no escaping the fact that Christianity means meeting the issues of everyday life head on and that is politics'.[59] So in as much as BMCs are articulating their interests, protecting their interests and expanding their interests and meeting the issues of everyday life head on they are being political.[60]

Also David Muir suggests that BMCs still look upon British Black theology with suspicion, but the reasons for this according to Muir are quite different from those outlined by Beckford. Muir[61] draws on the work of Nathan[62] who argues that the suspicion is based on the signifier 'Black' which lends itself to the assumption that there is a Black God for Black people and a White God for White people. For Nathan this is not the case. The problem seems to be finding an acceptable terminology to describe the theology. The signifier 'Black' is accepted by some BMCs and resented by others.[63] For Trotman the signifier reinforces discrimination and separation in the house of God and should be resisted. Finding an inclusive language, which is acceptable to all, appears to be impossible for reasons already noted. However, in his new book, Mark Sturge,[64] who was the former General Director of the African and Caribbean Evangelical Alliance has taken great pains to redeem the word 'Black' and to reclaim it as a positive term which adequately describes BMCs in Britain.

More significantly, the unpopularity of British Black theology in BMCs is a serious institutional problem, which is concerned with educational attainment among Black people in general, and theological education in particular. Muir had this to say on the issue: 'To a large extent [the] paucity of black British students in higher education in general and in theological education in particular, is one of the reasons why 'Black Theology' is relatively underdeveloped in Britain among [BMCs].'[65] Even where some BMCs have their own theological colleges, students suffer from lack of access to serious Black theological discourse and resources. In the forward to Gerloff's *A Plea for Black British Theologies*, Walter Hollenweger remarks: 'There is not even one specialist in any European or American university with a proper institute, library facilities, etc., to study the beginning of a new church which is happening under our noses.'[66] Additionally, Muir suggests that '[w]hile a few theological colleges were having short courses on "racism awareness", and even flirting with titles like "liberation" or "Black Theology", the majority remained culturally insular and theologically Eurocentric'.[67] Nathan is correct in his assessment that BMCs need to become proud of their culture, however that is understood.

Second, Beckford sees mixed heritage as a problem and accordingly he maintains that this makes it a difficult 'task of mobilizing under the banner of traditional, political Blackness'.[68] This argument seems far-fetched. The essential point is that the fragmentation of political Blackness was brought about by wider socio-political and economic factors to which mixed heritage appear to be peripheral. According to Sivanandan in an interview with Owusu, Black self-organization in the 1960s was 'an alternative to state integration'.[69] Collectively Black people (African, Asians and

African-Caribbean) had to fight against various forms of discrimination, racist immigration laws, the SUS laws and a number of other socio-political concerns. A number of self-help organizations were established to deal with those problems. In spite of this, the extinction of political Blackness was due to many factors including the rise of multiculturalism. For Sivanandan, the fragmentation of political Blackness was due

> partly [to] the race relation industry, partly the moneys (sic) thrown into the inner cities via Urban Aid and partly that Black unity broke down as Black ceased to be a political colour. With the coming of multiculturalism, Black British political identity ceded to African Caribbean and African and Asian cultural identities and separatism.[70]

This statement appears to suggest that the mixed heritage may have been an issue but that it is not as central as Beckford suggests.

Beckford's third argument is that of challenging the pneumatology of BMCs, and this is a more fundamental issue. For Beckford 'Black Majority Churches love to work and play with the Holy Spirit' but such excessive focus on pneumatology is in Beckford's view dangerous and unfortunate.[71] He writes: 'Unfortunately within many Black congregations, a distinction is made between a spiritual education and an academic education. Some believe that this spiritual education or intuitive-experiential learning is superior to an academic one.'[72] This again seems to reflect an argument that was in the past prevalent but which has now shifted so significantly that the claim can no longer be sustained.[73] The view that BMCs were more spiritually focused was according to Phillips 'created and nourished largely by the crude caricature of black American religion transmitted by Hollywood and television'.[74] The image, which was presented to the popular imagination, was that Black people in general were 'practising a form of barely understood fundamentalism which helps them escape into an imaginary world of the spirit'.[75]

Even more characteristically this perception is connected to '[t]he belief in the superiority of European values' which has been 'a basic element of European culture, and Christianity since the Middle Ages' and therefore '[t]o be Christian was to be white, and black Christians had to be apprentices to an entire range of European values'.[76] Some researchers continue to popularize this erroneous view without paying enough attention to recent trends in BMCs in Britain.

According to Mouw, 'life in the Spirit, properly understood, requires an active pursuit of justice'.[77] Therefore, Mouw argues, 'the active pursuit of justice desperately needs to be rooted in a conscious awareness of the power of the Holy Spirit'.[78] The focus on the Spirit was not to get to heaven but to address concrete socio-political issues in the here and now. Hollenweger writes of Asa Mahan:

> [It] was clear that he needed the 'power of the Holy Spirit' not 'to get to Heaven', nor 'to save souls', but in order to tackle concrete problems of politics and social morality . . . The philosophical, political and social endeavours of the Holiness evangelist were forgotten.[79]

Gerloff also comments on 'the revolutionary potential within early and later Black Pentecostalism'[80] which highlights the self-determination of the founders of the movement for radical engagement, which leads to the transformation of oppressive structures. William Seymour (1870–1922), an African-American, is regarded as the founder of the Azusa Street Pentecostal movement, which started in Los Angeles in 1906. According to Nelson, Seymour solved the race problem of the twentieth century. Nelson writes:

> In 1900 the famous black leader, W. E. B. Dubois, began writing prophetically, 'The problem of the Twentieth century is the problem of the color line'. When Seymour

provided the Azusa miracle to solve this problem he became the pre-eminent modern man for the century.[81]

On the other hand, 'many Black Christians are simple unaware of the socio-political motivations that produced their Christian tradition'.[82]

The crucial question is how to bridge the chasm among those who sit in pews, preach in pulpits and those who seek to propagate British Black theology. The following themes – celebration, dialogical relationships and critical and constructive criticism – are now outlined as possible ways of bridging the scholar–practitioner divide. Here I will use as an example, *Faith, Stories and the Experience of Black Elders* by Anthony Reddie to demonstrate how my three themes work together.

Celebration

The image of celebration is one of rejoicing, which marks a happy event and British Black theologies and the local churches and their leaders all have an equal part to play in this celebration. Theology itself, as Rowan Williams[83] states, begins as a celebratory process. Kabei Kirby, currently the General Manager of the African and Caribbean Evangelical Alliance, in an interview, remarks that much of the theologizing on BMCs in Britain tends to focus on problems rather than on a celebration of successes. Kirby believes that the successes of BMCs in Britain are not celebrated nearly enough. One of the dangers of celebration as Williams acknowledges is that it 'risk[s] "freezing" the reflective process and denying it the possibility of actively illuminating and modifying the concrete historical discourses of its environment, and of being renewed and extended by them'.[84] However, building a dialogical relationship coupled with critical and constructive criticism makes it unlikely that freezing will take place, thus creating the possibility for new ways of thinking and engaging.

Dialogical relationships

Louise Diamond states:

> Dialogue means we sit and talk with each other, especially those whom we may think we have the greatest differences. However, talking together all too often means debating, discussing with a view to convince the other, arguing for our point of view, examining pros and cons. In dialogue, the intention is not to advocate but to inquire; not to argue but to explore; not to convince but to discover.[85]

Diamond's definition of dialogue appears to lead to what Collins calls a dialogical relationship.[86] This is a relationship that leads to changing one's ways of thinking which in turn leads to changing one's actions or 'stimulat[ing] changed consciousness'.[87] Here, establishing a dialogical relation is not only crucial because it is concerned with arguing, advocating, debating, or trying to convince others but, as Pinn states, multidimensional dialogue involves rethinking the local in relation to wider global concerns.[88] By contrast, dialogue is focused on discovering, inquiring and exploring. This definition suggests a more open-minded approach to dialogue and in management vernacular it points to a 'win–win' solution where everyone benefits. This encourages what Cone calls an urge to interact, in spite of our difference.[89] The churches need to recognize, says Cone, the need for dialogue at local, national and international levels, which supports ecumenism. Roberts makes a similar point calling for more dialogue between the various strands of Black theologies throughout the world.[90]

This notion of establishing a dialogical relationship with others is perhaps what Williams refers to as a 'communicative' theology. This is a theology that is engaging with 'its uncommitted environment' and as a consequence is one that 'offers a way into fruitful conversation with the current

environment'.[91] According to Pinn, '[d]ialogue, not mono-
logues, is essential',[92] but this is a risky business. Engaging
with the unexamined aspects of beliefs is likely to uncover
thoughts that may result in a 'crisis' if what emerges is not
'identical or at least continuous with what has been believed
and articulated'.[93] A dialogical approach is crucial because it
opens up the way for critical and constructive criticisms for
dealing with any crisis that may result as a consequence of
engaging with difference.

Critical and constructive criticisms

According to Ira Brooks 'the church should be subjected to
healthy analysis and constructive criticism where necessary'.[94] The BMCs, in Brooks' view, are not above criticism
but where this takes place it must be constructive as well. To
be critical is to reflect on BMCs' commitment to justice for
themselves as well as for others.[95] There is another sense in
which one can be critical. 'Critical', according to Fairclough,
'implies showing connections and causes which are hidden; it
also implies intervention'.[96] Constructive criticism is useful
in helping people to see or better understand, in Foucault's
term, the 'power/knowledge relationship', which impacts
upon their lives.

Marx and Engels wrote: '[i]t is not the consciousness of
men that determines their being, but, on the contrary, their
social being that determines their consciousness'.[97] Likewise
Marx notes: '[t]he philosophers have only *interpreted* the
world, in various ways; the point however is to *change* it'.[98]
The task of critical and constructive criticism is to demonstrate how it is possible to live by consciousness and to break
away from the limiting social structures to create better
structures, which free people from want.

Anthony Reddie[99] like John Wilkinson, Nathan and others,
stresses the need to acknowledge and celebrate African-
Caribbean cultural identity. Central to Reddie's study, like
that of Gerloff was the need to document African-Caribbean

oral traditions in order to empower and inform African-Caribbean people. Importantly, Reddie's work has been an attempt to develop an intergenerational understanding for the inspiration, transformation and energizing of the younger generation of African-Caribbean Christians within the Methodist Church.

Reddie makes the point that it is important to remember that the contributions and achievements of the Black people and in particular the elders, is an ongoing process which should be constantly acknowledged and celebrated. Hence the aim of Reddie's study was to investigate the oral sources of Black experience. The aim was to use these traditions as a means of affirming Black elders living in Britain. The underlying idea behind this kind of research was to educate the young generation for the journeys ahead of them but also that the older generation might learn from the younger generation. In this context, Reddie has made a useful contribution in demonstrating how celebration, dialogical relationship and critical and constructive criticism work together in fostering meaningful change. Reddie's model could work at many levels and it has been well-tested in his Methodist community. This model comes highly recommended because it serves as a vehicle for bridging the gap between those who sit in pews, preach in pulpits and teach in academia. Like the apostle Paul who was travelling to distant lands to bring a message of hope to the people, so too Walter Rodney, as Noel Erskine points out, made it his duty to go to the homes of Rastas in Jamaica to educate them on the importance of Africa and its significance in world history. Like Paul and Walter Rodney, British Black theologians should follow suit and go to the people to teach and inform them. This is an important point. Gerloff suggests that an urgent issue which needs to be addressed is 'the unity of black theology and black empowerment, as promoted by the *Journal of Black Theology* in Britain, contextual, experiential and working for change'.[100] Considering the point made by Muir about access to education, and particularly theological education, it seems that the *Black Theology Journal* would have to do more than just gather articles and publish them. The hope is that more British Black theologians would participate in many of the regional and national conferences which BMCs have been running all over the country every year.

Conclusion

This chapter has suggested that by using the themes of celebration, dialogue, and critical and constructive engagement it is possible to bridge the gap among those who sit in pews, preach in pulpits and teach in seminaries. I want to end with a final quotation by Dorfman that reflects the need to fight on for an alternative vision of humanity.

> When a people attempt to liquidate centuries' worth of economic and social injustice, when they begin to gain a sense of their dignity as a nation (people), what is really at stake, what really inspires them, is an alternative vision of humanity, a different way of feeling and thinking and projecting and loving and keeping faith. And a different future.[101]

5. Images of Ministry: A Postcolonial Rereading

DAVID JOY

Introduction

Christianity and its mission in India is a very complex phenomenon as its history originated from the legend of the coming of the apostle Thomas to India in AD 52. Undoubtedly there was a Christian presence in the southern part of India in the early Christian centuries. Therefore many images and concepts used in the Church and its ministry have been linked up with the socio-political milieu of that time. However, with the arrival of Portuguese colonialism in 1498, those images were interwoven with colonialism. In this chapter, I will attempt to present a brief history of ministry and missionaries including biblical interpretation, looking at the condition of Christianity and society in general. In addition, I will take two major biblical images, namely 'grace' and 'kingdom of God' which had been used by the colonial mission schedule to ascribe an inferior status to the native people.

Missionaries, religion and colonialism

In this regard, it is worth noting that there was a nexus between the missionaries and the colonizers during the colonial period. Many studies in the field suggested that there were interconnections between culture and colonialism. However, local realities of indigenous institutions like *Vamsha* (lineage) and *Jati* (caste) were not redefined. Mission

and colonialism had been intrinsically connected, as emphasized by many historians and theologians of our time.
Vernacularization and Westernization happened simultaneously as mission and colonialism travelled together.

Isaac Padinjarekuttu, while analysing J. Schmidlin, a
German missiologist who lived in the first half of the twentieth century, stated that 'Mission has the task of conquering
the colonies spiritually. Only through this spiritual conquest
can the colonized peoples be made obedient and ready to
accept the external power of the colonizers.'[1] He has exposed
the situation that was created by the colonizers and the
missionaries who saw themselves as conquering the colonies
politically and spiritually. This attitude of the missionaries
unfortunately demolished the religio-cultural sentiments of
the natives in terms of their customs and practices. 'Con-
vinced that the conversion of India would lead to the conversion of Asia'[2] missionaries had sought the support of
British colonizers to achieve this goal. It was a mutually
beneficial business. The links between empire and religion
may be understood in the light of colonial history.

While examining the presence of the missionaries and
the Anglican Church in colonial India, Studdert-Kennedy
further stated that 'all these people were "intellectuals" in
the Gramscian sense, interpreting and underwriting a hegemonic ideology with pervasive religious undertones, which of
course functioned in support of the state and imperial structures'.[3] He argued that the natives thus felt the presence of the
missionaries to be part of the presence of the empire in their
situation.

In all areas of life the missionaries perpetuated a kind of
religious superiority. As a result even the very identity of the
Indian Christians had been questioned. At the same time,
the religious customs and practices of the subalterns and the
local people had been encouraged by some of the missionaries in order to ensure their support for colonial supremacy
by diminishing the conflict between the dominant religious
ideologies and the subalterns in the colonial context.

India: the contemporary context

It is very important to understand the historical and political background of India as a complex nation of many diverse religions and cultures. India's background now includes religious and cultural pluralism, fundamentalism, terrorism and the marginalization of women and Dalits. I propose to look at the culture and religions of India very briefly and then define the areas of caste and class. A study of the major shifts in the spread of Christianity will be helpful in understanding the various types of readings of the Bible.

Culture and religion

The spread of English literature promoted a new literary history in India which paved the way for a new and critical understanding of the local culture and religion. This critique emerged out of the painful memories of the ruthless massacres of native people by the Portuguese at the time of their invasion. In order to understand the religion and culture one should use an indigenous ethnography rather than the colonial ethnography because of its racist prejudices. European geographers and colonial historians kept the Eurocentric fabric in measuring the waves of Indian history without providing any space where the voice of the subalterns could be heard. The supremacy of the colonizers in terms of geographical knowledge enabled them to control India.[4]

The major stages of the spread of Christianity

The coming of Christianity had significant implications in the life and development of the local people. It is generally believed that great damage was done to the local cultures and civilizations. In 1955 Eddy Asirvatham wrote a book entitled *Christianity in the Indian Crucible*, a notable analysis and evaluation of the missionary strategies and the consequent damage done in terms of the local customs and practices.

However, in some areas it promoted the growth of the resistance movements of the lower caste people against their oppressors. Although the British government decided to support the caste system and used it to implement colonial rule, some London Missionary Society missionaries and Church Missionary Society missionaries questioned the evil practices and injustices of the caste system.[5]

Thus British colonialism made strategic shifts in the life and growth of the nations through missionaries, educators, industrialists and local collaborators. This resulted in many cultural and political struggles in India as people sought to establish or protect their religions and social identities. This situation caused serious paradigm shifts even in the area of biblical hermeneutics in India.

Indian hermeneutics: an overview

Even before the colonial missionary period, there were attempts among local Christian communities to interpret the Scriptures. However, those efforts were limited to the narrow framework of traditional teachings or doctrinal formulations. The following note from the website of the International Association for Mission Studies will explain the scenario clearly:

> A brief note is necessary concerning the large number of *Syriac and other manuscripts* which were written, copied and/or translated between 1504 and 1760, and which are still held in Kerala libraries. These include letters, Gospels, commentaries, liturgical MSS, apologies for the Church of the East and anthologies, from the third to fourteenth centuries. Amongst many Indian writers, copyists and compilers recorded in MS colophons are *Mar Jacob* (1504), *Jacob Malpan* 'of Malabar' (1556), *Mar Joseph* (1567), *Mattai Panorkidan* (1584), *Metropolitan Simon* (1701), *Deacon Abraham of Mudurute* (1734) *Mar Iwannis* (1749), and *Jacob Julius* (Konat) (c. 1790).[6]

This reference indicates that for most of the commentators of that time, interpretation meant simply explaining the doctrinal insights in the texts. A successful tracing back of the biblical interpretation from the history of the Indian Christianity since the first century AD is not necessary, because the interpretations were centred around mere doctrinal explanations.

Colonial period

Colonialism had influenced the missionary articulation of Christian faith. Eventually it determined the question of identity. Correspondingly, Jayakiran Sebastian thinks that 'one cannot forget the legacy of colonialism, which resulted in massive ferment at various levels of society, and also resulted in different groups within society attempting to forge new patterns of relational identity'.[7] But in that era the biblical exegetes approached the Bible with a literal interpretation which left out the cultural elements of the native people. This was done in the shadow of the missionary pattern of hermeneutics. At the same time there were some attempts by native biblical scholars/interpreters such as A. J. Appasamy to understand the Bible in accordance with their cultural framework. Bishop V. S. Azariah of Dornakal made substantial contributions in this regard. Moreover the impact of the missionaries in higher education in India inspired a fresh study of Scripture, though it was once again a copy of the Western evangelistic pattern, based more or less on the assumption of the 'superior' status of Christianity. Nevertheless, two main patterns of biblical interpretation can be categorized, namely colonialist readings and native indigenous readings.

By the same token, the Bible was utilized by the missionaries to inculcate their values and customs, which resulted in the displacement of the local cultures. Moreover, the process of overtextualization created an atmosphere of hostility among the native religions. The series of commentaries pro-

duced by the Anglican Church in India for the Indians since
1890 showed the pattern of interpretation during that time.
There were nine commentaries, and all were published by
SPCK Depository, Madras. The writers of those commentaries were well-accepted Western scholars such as J. B.
Lightfoot, B. F. Westcott, and F. J. A. Hort. These commentaries were also translated into vernacular languages. R. S.
Sugirtharajah, after a careful evaluation of these commentaries, states:

> The commentaries seek out and identify what they deem to
> be evils of Indian society: superstition, mendacity, laziness
> and bribery; all of these have to be resisted. In setting such
> moral boundaries between Indian Christians and other
> Indians, the commentaries served to establish the case for
> the British intervention. By prescribing Christian morality,
> these commentaries became the textual means for justify-
> ing the British occupation as the harbinger of civilization.[8]

Thus these commentaries caused divisions, hatred and
hostility among the native people in terms of their education
and social status. In this connection a number of similar
expositions prepared and published by the missionaries
may be noted.[9] Edward Sell's commentary on the Psalms,
'written primarily for the Indian clergy', again portrayed the
Christian religion as a superior one when compared with the
native religious customs and practices. In 1927, L. P. Larsen
wrote a monograph, *Christ's Way and Ours*, containing a
number of Bible studies urging the natives (local people) to
'trustful dependence on God and humble acknowledgement
of His power and blessing are indispensable if His kingdom
is to come and to grow' (83). Even in a book entitled *Village
Preaching* by James I. Macnair, the then principal of the
United Telugu Seminary in 1924, there was no serious contribution in terms of recognizing the local values and customs. Rather, it copied the purview of Eurocentric biblical
interpretation.

Since the missionary pattern of hermeneutics did not give adequate recognition and respect to the native culture and customs, the postcolonial biblical hermeneutics respects the culture and heritage of the local people as well as exposing connections between race, nation, the translation of the text, mission and colonialism. The postcolonial interpretation of the Bible stems from the resistant, heritagist, nationalist and liberationist readings which affirmed the fact that no culture is superior or inferior to another.[10]

A postcolonial biblical reading

In the light of these findings, it is argued that a postcolonial biblical hermeneutics may enable the readers of the Bible to understand the meaning of the images of ministry used by the interpreters in a postcolonial context. Since the 'post' implies periodization, the second half of the twentieth century can be called postcolonial. Therefore the focus would be the issues and concerns posed during this time. In 2005 Stephen. D. Moore and Fernando F. Segovia edited a book entitled *Postcolonial Biblical Criticism: Interdisciplinary Intersections* (the sixth book in the series 'The Bible and Postcolonialism') and this volume is a major contribution to the field of postcolonial biblical criticism. The editors claim:

> This volume carefully positions postcolonial biblical criticism in relation to other important political and theoretical currents in contemporary biblical studies: feminism; racial/ethnic studies; poststructuralism; and Marxism. Alternating between hermeneutical and exegetical reflection, the essays cumulatively isolate and evaluate the definitive features of postcolonial biblical criticism.[11]

Segovia argues that such postcolonial biblical criticism should take insights from other disciplines into account when the Bible is read. He writes:

Such study, I would argue, should: foreground throughout the unequal relationship of domination and subordination at work; address the imperial as well as the colonial spaces, the center and the periphery; examine both cultural production and material matrix; make room for pursuing colonial in its own terms; and opt for diversity in recording the encounter between the imperial and the colonial. Finally, given its own emphasis on a relationship of equality, such study should affect and be affected by other studies with a similar focus on unequal relations – Feminist, Liberation, Minority, Gay and Lesbian studies. A tall order, indeed, but of the essence.[12]

He has argued that a critical use of insights from every available contextual readings is necessary for a fruitful exercise of postcolonial biblical interpretation.

Images of ministry

In the context of colonial links with the ministry and mission of the Church in India many images and concepts used need to be reworked with the help of insights from postcolonial studies. I will look into the details of two images, namely grace and kingdom of God as both have been linked with a superior position of the Christian religion in a postcolonial context.

Grace

Deriving from the Greek word *charis*, it offers a variety of meanings such as grace, graciousness, favour, thanks, gratitude and others. In the New Testament milieu, *charis* not only refers to the attitude of God, but also designates the dispensations of the emperor.[13] However, Jesus uses *charis* to denote an understanding of protection offered to the weak, poor, hopeless, women and despised ones (Matt. 11.5, 28; Mark 10.26ff; Luke 15).[14]

In the light of this brief note, I wish to examine the understanding of *charis* by two contemporary biblical readers, namely Leonardo Boff and Elza Tamez. Leonardo Boff defines *charis* within the contextual and historical realities of a person and community. He states: 'Grace is not something mysterious in the sense of being impalpable. Grace is the personal, living presence of God in life itself, dwelling there to make it more fully life, more fully open to heaven and earth alike.'[15] In the same way, Elsa Tamez argues that *charis* of God will strengthen the weak, the poor will receive the good news, and the sick and needy will be healed.[16] Leonardo Boff's 1981 book *Liberating Grace* is a classic piece of literature that deals with *charis* in a deeper manner. According to him *charis* is understood as faith, hope, love, friendship, peace, joy, a critical spirit, courage, among other things.[17] Therefore, it is argued that *charis* has multidimensional meanings in the contemporary socio-political and religio-cultural contexts. Hence, a postcolonial feminist reading of a biblical text may reveal some of the hidden meanings of this word to our postcolonial context and to the maternal face of God. Grace should be counted as a property of mission and colonial authorities as many of the contemporary *prosperity gospel* preachers present the issue. In a postcolonial context historical realities of suffering and subjugation should be taken into account while defining grace. Thus *charis* truly becomes a divine act through human channels to introduce justice and peace to this world.

Kingdom of God

The kingdom of God has always been linked with a privilege offered to a dominant group. Thus it was misused to subjugate the people of 'the other' religion, gender, race and ethnicity. For instance, a healing story in Mark 5.1–20 is interpreted by the traditional readers of the text as the one event which counts only a dominant group special. Here, the dominant group means an affluent group that controls the power and authority. Similarly, there are many recent studies which place this text and similar passages in Mark dealing with the themes of purity, demons and evil spirits in the 'healing-mission' framework. Similarly, Nineham reads the text as if there were a divinely ordained division which favoured only a chosen group.[18]

This was exactly the point the missionaries wanted to stress – that the natives were inferior. This pattern of interpretation is in some way hostile in a multireligious context. During the colonial and postcolonial period in India most of the interpreters endorsed this traditional interpretation believing that the inclusion of the Gentiles should happen even at the expense of their culture and native religious practices.

Unfortunately the traditional exegetes did not look at the pains and agonies of the demon-possessed man or the domination of the Roman colonial system. Overemphasis on the demoniac offered by the traditional interpretations encouraged the misunderstanding of native cultures and customs as demonic. The blind neglect of this presence of the empire in the text is a fundamental failure and limitation of the traditional commentators. By branding the native customs, festivals and practices as demonic the traditional commentators ridiculed the voice of 'the other'.

A postcolonial reading will enable the readers to unmask the oppressive systems and help the subalterns to understand the position of the oppressor. The presence of empire in the text as well as in the context will be recognized by these interpretations and thus colonialism will be brought to the centre of biblical interpretation. Marcella Althaus-Reid's study is an arresting one as it deals with the voices of the *Fracasados* who represent the marginalized groups in Argentina, including street children, the unemployed and the slum-dwellers. Being people of the margins, their reading of the text could be a postcolonial one. It consists of orality, marginal experience, a decentring of the religious experience and the recognition of otherness.[19] The kingdom of God in this context should be a wider and broader one including the voices and aspirations of the marginalized and the oppressed people.

Arundhati Roy, a winner of the Booker prize, in her masterpiece novel *The God of Small Things*, beautifully and brilliantly presents the inner dynamics and shifts in the family relations and social life of postcolonial Kerala. Roy thinks that colonialism preserves its neocolonial links with native intellectuals, upper-caste people and the multinational corporations.

The present understanding of the kingdom of God has posed a number of vital questions about the pattern and purview of the Christian mission in the postcolonial context. These institution-centred endeavours at redefinition will not be fruitful in the postcolonial context, unless and until the multiplicity of voices are taken into account. Marion Grau says that 'the heavenly basileia Jesus knew ever more closely resembled the power structures of the terrestrial Roman Empire'.[20] Similarly, the ideology of mission and evangelization resembled the colonial empire; hence an atmosphere of suspicion prevailed.

Conclusion

This chapter has attempted to present some issues linked with the interpretation of key images of ministry in a post-colonial Indian context. The imperial presence in the interpretations should not be overlooked by the readers of the Bible. Therefore, it is the task of the interpreter to present the biblical message without the imprint of the imperial schema. Thus it is necessary to scrutinize the use of images of ministry and mission in a postcolonial context.

6. Black Theology, Englishness and the Church of England

DAVID ISIORHO

Towards a Black Anglican theology of liberation

A Black Anglican theology of liberation should look two ways: into the past to discover how the present identity and self-awareness of the Church of England has evolved, taking into account the colonial past and the inheritance of racialized patterns of behaviour and racism; it should look forward to discover how a new understanding of English ethnicity can transform the Church of England into a dynamic and inclusive community.

The state religion of the UK is Christianity as it is expressed in the Church of England and it continues to be an important signifier of Englishness. A Black Anglican theology of liberation is about the mode of inclusion in the UK of Black communities and their response to divine activity within that institution. Anglicanism is often described as the local expression of the Christian Church in a given place. The Church of England has no special doctrines of its own but rather proclaims the historic faith of the Christian Church. But what is the relationship between Anglicanism grounded in the historical formularies of the Church of England and its Black worshippers? What is the Black God-talk here and what are the structures for dialogue and inclusion?

I find that the Church of England is currently just as much concerned with ethnicity as it is with theism. Thus the mode of involvement of Black Anglicans is motivated and driven by a political agenda that can be found in English ethnicity.

This chapter explores the implications for Church and nation within a context of postdiasporic identities. The celebration of diversity within Anglicanism can be seen as an expression of Englishness, but ecclesiastical diversity is not to be confused with cultural inclusiveness.

Racial justice issues are marginalized and seen as controversial, along with women bishops and homosexuals. Thus a Black Anglican liberation theology will need to identify a relationship between English ethnicity and institutionalized racism.

Defining Englishness

So how can we define what it is to be English within the context of contemporary British culture? What distinctions should be made between Anglo-Saxon and Celtic communities? It is common for writers in this field to use the term 'British' as a generic to include English, Welsh, Scottish and Irish experience. However, distinctions are made when the English are accused of defining the UK as English. This line of argument is used to draw attention to the conflicts between the historic nationality groups that make up the UK.

English identity, although not easily defined, is usually seen as the most dominant. The idea here is that Wales, Ireland and Scotland somehow construct their own identity in hostile reaction to the English. This in turn leads to a collection of stereotypes in which the English are portrayed as calm, reasonable, patient and above all in complete contrast to the Celts who are excitable and impulsive. Further English attributes include tolerance, decency, moderation, consensus and compromise, with an emphasis upon modesty. The Celts, however, do not perceive the English as restrained and reserved but rather as arrogant, cold and patronizing. There is also an idea that the English cherish the vocation of the amateur and the eccentric along with a very dry sense of humour characterized by understatement.

This literature does not usually include Cornish or Manx

groups as distinct entities within a broad category such as English or Irish. Regional dimensions are usually avoided as they are likely to complicate arguments. I believe that these cross-cultural and geographical factors are crucial to an understanding of English identities even if they suggest a fractured UK with as many divisions within nationality groups as between them. However, the whole debate about citizenship has not come about as a result of these divisions but because of claims that immigration has been detrimental to national identity, which is really about the preservation of Whiteness in the UK and the lament of empire.

The role of Protestantism in defining European identities

Whiteness as a signifier of European identity is a category that represents dominance, normality and privilege and, as such, can be identified historically with Protestantism. The starting point of this discussion is to be found in a recognition that the concept of Whiteness becomes increasingly more specialized and specific when applied to Englishness and is a signpost to its geographical and ecclesiastical isolation.

It can be argued that England exchanged its European identity for a British identity during the colonial expansion of the nineteenth century, which was also the time of missionary activity. The British colonized huge tracts of land and were not seriously challenged by any cultural cousin until World War One. The British Empire meant that the English were isolated and estranged from the rest of Europe, which accounts to some extent for the defensive, reactive nature of English identity through which Anglicanism had already become a repository of oppression.

We can link this to an understanding of Englishness as a cultural system, in opposition to Continental Catholicism, and so to its implications for the relationship between African-Caribbean communities in the Church of England.

The British had four centuries in which to distrust Catholics who happened to be French, Spanish and Italian. In so doing, they united a kingdom of White groups who previously described themselves as regional variants of English, Irish, Scottish and Welsh origin. By the time African-Caribbean people came to the UK in significant numbers in the 1950s, the British already knew how to exclude them from the institutions of White society, which included the Church of England.

Deconstructing Whiteness and the New Right

For the New Right, Englishness is the same thing as Whiteness and, as such, becomes the defining term making any thing associated with Black a dependent category. Whiteness is culturally constructed as a concealed category with no consciousness of its own, but existing asymmetrically and implicitly in opposition to others. Thus, tapping into Western thought and language, the New Right are able to use this construction of Englishness as a cultural marker against which everything else is defined as foreign and not belonging.

Englishness in this context is a privileged signifier that marginalizes Black people as that 'other'. White people are under no pressure to identify with their cultural Whiteness because it is perceived to be the norm. Englishness in association with Whiteness does not have to explain itself to itself nor to anyone else for that matter. The closer English identities are to Whiteness, the more difficult it is to see any substantive ideas lying behind them; which as a corollary, leads to this construct being infused with notions of contradiction and fragmentation.

The disintegration of Englishness can be seen in imaginary dramas and narratives. It is evidenced in the way in which the English represent England to themselves as 'cucumber sandwiches', 'tea on the lawn', and 'spinsters cycling to evensong'. This has often involved the Church as a recurrent provider of caricatures and characters in English literature and the arts. Thus two recurrent themes in popular culture have been the comic potential of clergy and the sense of departure from the certainties of the past. A link can be made between the English novel and Patrick Wright's concept of a *Deep England* that never existed except in the selective memory of the privileged.[1] Thus, the world of English literature is a signpost to a Deep Anglicanism, which is pre-occupied with its past and with itself. As an icon of Englishness, the Church of England continues to have an influential role within the life of the nation simply because it is able to represent England to the English. This is shown clearly on state occasions when national loyalty is combined with implicit religion.

This is about religion acting as a boundary marker, distinguishing the true English Protestant from a Catholic foreigner. Coronations and royal weddings are set-piece occasions on which the Church of England provides state rituals that express a boundary-making principle. Mrs Thatcher went to Westminster Abbey, not Westminster Cathedral, to 'celebrate' the victory in the Falklands. It is in Westminster Abbey that England buries its ancient and great. Historically the Church of England had a very particular position in relation to constructed Englishness and, until recently, a very high profile was maintained. Today, while the centrality of the Church within the life of the nation has been weakened, it is still possible to argue that the Church continues to be an important signifier of Englishness.

Racism-awareness training and the Anglican mode of liberation

Having defined Englishness and its relationship to Whiteness we now need to clarify the pattern of attitudes within the institution of the Church of England that convey racism and institutional racism that affects the whole Church of God. And for this reason some very basic questions have to be asked. For example, are Black people more welcome in our urban churches than in the countryside? How easy is it for Black parishioners to be elected on to the PCC (Parochial Church Council – the place of oversight and decision-making in the local Anglican Church) or to become a churchwarden? How are Black clergy deployed in our church? Are more Black clergy sent to cities rather than to rural parishes and are they overlooked when it comes to promotion to positions of greater responsibility in our church?

There is no uniformity between the 44 dioceses of the Church of England with respect to racism-awareness training and little or no co-ordination from the centre. The sum total of what is done can be described as a 'palace of variety' with some dioceses providing training for all staff, while some have training for senior staff and others have none at all. Some dioceses do racism-awareness training as part of diversity training across cultures, and claim to include race equality legislation and even address the issue surrounding the appropriate use of language. However, oftentimes, the concern around appropriate language use is reduced to the idea of avoiding using the word 'race' or racism on the grounds that these terms may cause offence. This is a very serious neglect of responsibility on the part of those who should know better and can only alienate Black support for the Church.

Learning about other cultures and treating them with empathy is in theory an effective challenge to racism, but this is not substantiated by empirical evidence. This approach underestimates the existence of racial prejudice and discrimination. Britain has always been a multicultural society in the sense that its inhabitants do not embrace a monolithic set of values and experience. If culture is defined to include class, gender and religion, then it is obviously more multicultural than most people would want to acknowledge.

Clearly the multiculturalists have a racialized concept of culture. By cultural they mean the lifestyles that are associated with racial designations. When they say Britain is a multicultural society what they mean is that some of its inhabitants embrace a way of life that is different from that of the White British.

Good practice can be seen in only a handful of Church of England dioceses which have adopted a racism-awareness strategy that seeks to make crucial connections between theology, spirituality and issues of racism which affect people outside of church structures. These dioceses have employed full-time staff to oversee this work. This training is sometimes called 'Awareness Training: Racism'. The thinking here is to make the point that there are other forms of oppression such as sexism and homophobia to which a response should also be made.

Racism-awareness training must include a strong anti-racist element. It is racism that determines life chances, not lifestyles. Many decades of multiculturalism have done very little to stem the tide of racism. Training for racial equality must include direct teaching about racism.

Recommendations

The quest for an English identity that leaves behind the colonial past and the British identity of Empire involves a process of change which many Anglicans will find difficult. It involves an explicit realization of the Christian faith that takes the mission and the maintenance work of the Church out of the subjective realm into a more concrete arena, thus enabling the old Anglican virtue of reason to function. We need to critique and dialogue with current praxis against a prophetic and biblical backdrop. We do this within a framework of church theology that embraces all the traditional aspects of the work and mission of the Church from its earliest inception.

I conclude this chapter with a series of recommendations to the Church of England that focus upon a relationship between institutionalized racism and English ethnicity. The recommendations are presented in the context of the four primary purposes of Church:

1 worship and prayer;
2 teaching and nurture;
3 evangelism and outreach;
4 justice and care.

Note the movement from the internal to the communal and to the global in these four categories. The lure of the private in English Anglicanism is very strong.

Worship and prayer

The Church of England should take seriously the role of Englishness in the life and worship of Black Anglicans since it is this, and not individual choice and inclination, that determines their mode of involvement. If the Church wants to increase Black involvement, then it must stop putting the responsibility for involvement on Black worshippers and look instead to the institution in which that involvement would take place.

The Church of England should recognize that the mode of involvement of Black Anglicans within the Afro-Caribbean community is likely to be influenced by family group membership, where the Anglican Church is seen as the norm, not adult conversion. The liturgy should reflect this while, at the same time, embracing innovation and diversity within that normality.

Teaching and nurture

The Church of England should abandon its *race relations* approach to challenging racism. The idea that teaching people about each others' cultures, by itself, can eradicate racial discrimination in the Church and in society is not supported by the research evidence. *Race relations* must be replaced by an approach which contains a strong anti-racist component. Racial awareness training must be *racism* awareness training. Understanding of ourselves must go beyond personal relations to encompass power relations within the institution of the Church.

The concept of institutionalized racism must not be used as a means of abdicating responsibility for racially discriminatory behaviour on the part of congregations, clergy or senior managers.

Evangelism and outreach

The Church of England should conduct an audit of its financial and human resources to see what proportion of diocesan budgets relates to issues of (a) racial justice and (b) Black involvement.

The Church should identify its future leadership among Black clergy and ensure that their potential for leadership is appropriately nurtured. This will involve giving advice, guidance and career counselling, to empower Black clergy and ensure that they have the opportunities to work in varied settings within the Church and to gain the necessary experience to compete for senior management positions on the same basis as White clergy.

Black clergy should have the opportunity for serving Black or White congregations. Bishops should be aware that urban and industrial parishes are not the only places where Black clergy are likely to be accepted. It may well be the case that the larger rural parish where the vicar is still 'the vicar' (in the traditional all-encompassing sense of the term) is where the Church would be able to normalize the presence of Black clergy.

The Church should seek to foster and encourage Black non-stipendiary clergy who work in secular settings. It should also offer them the opportunity of working full-time if they feel vocationally called to do so.

The Church of England should theologize from within the global Anglican experience and interpret the meaning of the Christian faith in a way that takes into account the perspective of Black Christians.

The Church of England should welcome, wholeheartedly, the intervention of other Anglican churches and see itself as a field for missionary activity, that is the movement from the so-called 'rest to the West', or mission in reverse!

The Church should stop talking about Black participation for this denotes Black people fitting into a White organization. Rather, evangelism within the African-Caribbean community should be about involvement which is both significant and meaningful. The concept of involvement suggests a partnership and some convergence of perspective.

Justice and care

The Church of England should appoint more specialist officers from among Black clergy, even if this means withdrawing them from parochial settings. This should be seen as a rationalizing and professionalizing of the Church's resources and not as a drain on our existing human capital. The *inner-city* churches cannot go on being funded without serious reorganization of human resources.

The Church of England must recruit from its able Black clergy staff in order that they can serve in the middle management positions of archdeacon, cathedral canon, cathedral dean, bishop's chaplain, social responsibility officer and team rector. Black candidates should be included on all long lists for middle and senior office holders.

The Church should take seriously its management function and introduce a proper criterion for certification. There should be examinations as a precondition for the appointment to the office of archdeacon, cathedral canon, cathedral dean, bishop's chaplain, social responsibility officer; team rector, suffragan bishop, area bishop and diocesan bishop.

Conclusion

The Church of England can be described as a repository of contemporary oppression because the interface between

Church and state is exemplified in Anglican support for colonialism. The Church of England welcomed the conquest of non-European lands by the colonial powers, seeing in this process an opportunity for evangelism. The colonial expansion of the nineteenth century left behind a religious legacy that contributed to the alienation of postcolonial societies. I have tried to understand the role of Protestantism in defining European identity by exploring the possibility that the religious conflict between British Protestants and European Catholics dating back to the sixteenth century laid the foundation for later conflicts involving indigenous UK populations and those seen as outsiders.

The Church of England should seek to establish a greater connection between what it says about racial justice issues and what it actually does. It should demonstrate its willingness to do this by means of a major reorganization of its financial and human resources. It follows that the Church of England should only maintain the parochial structures in situations of greatest viability. This may mean closing down some parishes and collapsing others in order to divert resources to chaplaincy-style interventions and the appointment of more specialist staff.

The Church of England should welcome the efforts of Black Anglicans to caucus and to seek some measure of empowerment in response to their marginalized status. The career of Black clergy should be as jealously and assiduously protected as that of favoured White clergy. As the established Church, the Church of England has a peculiarly strong influence on the wider Anglican Communion. Black Anglicanism should reclaim the apostolic and catholic fundamentals of the tradition in order to achieve two related goals: the reinvigoration of the Anglican Church and the integrity of the Church's mission in the world as a major force for justice as well as for salvation. It is important, therefore, for Black Anglicanism to look at what it means to be a member of the universal Church.

7. Out of Every Tribe and Nation: The Making of the Caribbean Diasporan Church

DELROY A. REID-SALMON

Introduction

This chapter seeks to discover the identity of the Caribbean diasporan church by examining how Caribbean people understand themselves in order to define the theological identity of the church and thereby construct a theology of the identity that will guide, inform and sustain faith and the practice of ministry in a new and strange land. In developing this theological self-understanding, I will consider the pan-Caribbean identity as the foremost Caribbean diasporan identity. It is based on faith and mediated or embodied through ethnicity and the common history and experience of Caribbean immigrants.

Since the Caribbean varies in culture, geography and population and is diverse in race/ethnicity, the term 'pan-Caribbean' describes the people from the countries known as the Commonwealth Caribbean or the former British colonies which have a common heritage and experience of slavery, British colonialism and United States imperialism.[1] The term symbolizes the meaning of life, values and identity forged out of the diasporan experience. It represents continuity with the past, creation of identity and community. As such, hyphenated names like Caribbean-American, African-Caribbean are used to provide a sense of history and identity. The term is also used as a symbol of Caribbean unity and emancipation in the struggle against injustice. Consequently, in the diaspora, Caribbean people replace their national identity with the all-inclusive term 'pan-Caribbean'. This, however, does not simplify the meaning of the identity.

Diasporan identity and existence are problematic issues. In my initial discussions about the Caribbean diaspora, my conversants expressed either uninterest, dismay or disregard for the subject. I recalled being told bluntly in my earliest discussions that there is no such thing as a Caribbean diaspora. In subsequent discussions, I was asked about the value of defining and referring to Caribbean people living in foreign countries as a diaspora and if it is not a way of separating them from the others of African descent. They asked: Is this another attempt to create an ethnic enclave and ghetto? Will this self-identity not alienate us from other people groups? Why is it important to have this identity?

What is true and cannot be disputed is that we all come from somewhere else to be where we are. Addressing this issue, the social philosopher, Stuart Hall, states:

> The Caribbean is the first, the original and the purest diaspora. These days blacks who completed the triangular journey back to Britain sometimes speak of the emerging black British diaspora, but I have to tell them that they and I are twice diasporized. Furthermore, we are not just living in a diaspora where the center is always somewhere else, but we are the break with those originating cultural sources as passed through the traumas of violent rupture.[2]

Why is diaspora problematic? It is a very complex issue at the centre of public life in a rapidly changing world. The certainties, sense of identity and unity that once characterized societies died with the advent of globalization. Consequently, alienation, fragmentation, instability coupled with transnational economic, social and communication trends have redefined and transformed the meaning of identity, ethnicity, nationality and culture. Diaspora contends with these global hegemonic forces and addresses also the issues of space, time and new realities. Moreover, diaspora is essentially not about geography, group solidarity or community formation. These are, however, some of the reasons that make understanding diaspora and having a diasporan identity problematic.

These problems evoke questions such as: What does it mean to live in a strange land? Who are we, when we are uprooted, dispersed and displaced from our homeland, whether through coercion or volition? What is the meaning of the diasporan experience and what does it mean to be a diasporan people? A theological interpretation of the Caribbean diaspora seeks to discover the collective meaning of the diasporan experience. The experience produces a people. But what is the basis on which Caribbean diasporan experience makes a people? I argue that it is the making of a people on the basis of faith in Jesus Christ mediated through the self-understandings of pan-Caribbean identity which is grounded in the incarnation of Jesus Christ and the event of Pentecost. In this regard, I will argue that faith is the basis of a Caribbean diasporan identity represented through the Caribbean diasporan church as a pan-Caribbean community of faith. With this understanding, the discussion will define the meaning of diaspora, explore the formation of the pan-Caribbean identity and delineate the theological basis of this identity.

Diaspora: meaning and contents

The meaning of diaspora evolves. In the classic usage, it describes the dispersing or scattering of the Jewish people during the Old Testament era. The term originally means to sow, scatter, disperse, disseminate. R. S. Sugirtharajah in trying to define the term argues that it describes the dispersion and deportation experience of the Jewish people who lived outside Palestine.[3] The term is also used to describe the Christian experience during the first century. The Christians understood themselves as God's new people through whom God's promises were going to be fulfilled.

> The Christian Church is seen as the wondering pilgrim and a disperse community, in the sense that they are the instruments to fulfill Gods' eschatological purpose. The home they were striving for is not an earthly home but a home which is above and yet to come . . . On earth Christian living in dispersion would function as the seed in disseminating the message of Jesus.[4]

Sugiratharajah is careful to note that these Christians were not exiles in the contemporary understanding of the term. As the people of Christ, they had a sense of catholicity about their faith and life. According to Sugiratharajah, 'They knew they were living in a distinct way which had wider global and salvational significance.'[5] He goes further in making a very important observation about the amnesia of the Christians after they become a part of the status-quo or members of the dominant culture. 'After acquiring institutional status, however, the early Christian movement slowly forgot this notion of a sojourning, wandering people of God with transnational connection.'[6] He calls for a closer attention to this changing posture. 'Once a marginal community and seen as a perfect paradigm for provisional sojourning spirit, the Christian community had gradually lost its subalternity, moving into the centre.'[7]

The meaning of diaspora is not limited to the biblical understanding. It transcends the biblical Jewish paradigm to include the indescribable genocide of the Atlantic Slave Trade that began in the sixteenth century. It was a forced migration of Africans from their homeland to the so-called New World consisting of North and South America and the Caribbean. The term 'diaspora' is used to describe this experience.

One of the consequences of this legalized slavery of over 400 years, is the formation of various of Black diasporas.

The diversity of the Black diaspora is a result of the variety of sources from which the people came; that includes different societies, ethnic groups and cultures and the different places where they were brought. In other words, from where they came and where they went formed the foundation of what constitutes the Black diaspora. These peoples, however, are homogeneous in having a common origin, formation and experience: Africa, the Western world and oppression.[8]

In recent times the term 'diaspora' has assumed a new meaning. It changes from identification with the biblical people to an interpretative account of the migration experience. As a signifier of this change in meaning of diaspora, concerned scholars created in 1991 the journal, *Diaspora: A Journal of Transnational Studies*. In the inaugural issue, the founding editor, Khachig Tololyan, comments, 'immigrant, expatriate, refugee, guest worker, exile community' are elements of diaspora.[9] These migrant people are becoming a community but are in the middle of nowhere and are on the margins of the dominant society. In this regard, William Safran defines diaspora as the

Segment of people living outside their homeland and having a collective memory, vision or myth about their original homeland . . . believe that they are not fully accepted by their host society and feel partially alienated from it and where the true home is the ancestral home, where there is commitment to work for its development and whose identity is defined by this sense of home.[10]

Safran observes the ambivalence and ambiguities of diasporan existence by pointing out some of the dangers diasporan communities face, such as material success, which has the potential to weaken ethnic identity, and the notion of 'homeland' which, rather than being a historical existence, is an eschatological construct to cope with the reality of diasporan existence.[11]

The challenge of living with such ambiguities is what

Robin Cohen demonstrates in his attempt to define diaspora using the Caribbean diaspora as a model. In Safran's model, there is an emphasis on victimhood implicit in the notion of forced movement. For Cohen, diaspora is a voluntary movement in search of a better life. In another departure from Safran, who defines diaspora in terms of its relationship with the homeland, Cohen defines diaspora on the basis of culture.[12] He argues that diasporan communities have to do more than maintain their homeland but to create their own identity based on heritage, history and memory.[13] These factors – dispersal from homeland, memory and commitment to its maintenance, return movements, community identity, ambivalent relationship with host country and having a better life – constitute a diaspora which Cohen defines in the metaphorical usage of a rope of which these are its fibres.[14]

Cohen's definition of diaspora also departs from the biblical-identification model to embrace an existential understanding consistent with the literal meaning of the term as dispersion and growth which is described as an exilic experience. The term 'exile' denotes displacement, oppression, homelessness, alienation, sin, remorse, shame, marginality, emancipation and hope. As such, it is a place of ambiguities and contradictions. George Lamming in *The Pleasures of Exile* depicts such a view of the Caribbean diaspora. The title indicates the author's self-understanding and the relationship between identity and locality. Life in exile is a perennial struggle between death and life, separation and reconciliation, oppression and emancipation, rejection and belonging, hate and love. On the one hand life is undesirable and on the other hand, it is pleasurable.

What then is exile? Is it a place of choice or coercion? When will emancipation take place and on what basis can the exiles live in hope? The oppressor is identified but who is the liberator? These questions are left unanswered. Contrary to the biblical understanding of emancipation, in Lamming's view, exile is a place of choice. Lamming writes: 'I do believe that what a person thinks is very much determined by the way that person sees. The book is really no more than a report of one man's way of seeing, using certain facts of experience and as guide.'[15] Also, exile for Lamming is a good place. It is a place not of sorrow but of celebration. He writes, 'to be an exile is to be alive'.[16]

The exilic metaphor does not take into account the ambiguities and ambivalences of the experience. Moreover it advocates an assimilationist posture. There is also the danger of sanitizing the people and characters whose actions over time led to a reverse in the experience. For example, in the case of Nehemiah, he and his colleagues administered one of the most brutal treatments to the natives of the country (Ezra 9–10). The actions reveal some of the limitations of exile as the ideal paradigm for defining diaspora. This uncritical use of the Bible indicates that a diasporan identity is yet to be developed.

There is another change in the meaning of diaspora. Black theologians understand it as a source for theological discourse. Black British theologian Robert Beckford argues in his *Dread and Pentecostal: A Political Theology for the Black Church in Britain*, that the Caribbean diasporan experience is a source for doing Black theology.[17] How is the diaspora a source for doing theology? Any authentic Black theology seeks to address the issues that come out of its context. Using William Safran's criteria of defining and analysing a diaspora, Beckford explores six areas of concern or issues that emerge out of the Caribbean diaspora experience.[18] These issues are 'Dispersal from an Original Centre', 'Maintaining a Memory', 'Never Accepted by their Hosts', 'The Ancestral Home as a Place of Eventual Return', 'Restoring the Homeland' and 'Group Solidarity'.[19]

Beckford's interpretation is an initial attempt to give theological meaning to the Caribbean diaspora. It indicates where Black theology breaks from and is different from Euro-American theology. The former begins with experience and the latter begins with metaphysics. This further introduces a new methodology in doing theological reflection and shows the value of human experience. The Beckfordian interpretation, however, does not provide any theological meaning to the experience. Also, this view leaves un-answered the question as to the theological meaning of the issues and concerns that emerge. In other words, the Caribbean diasporan experience as a source for theological discourse should provide a theological interpretation of the issues and concerns of the diaspora and seeks to answer the question, 'What do these issues mean in light of the gospel of Jesus Christ?'

Diasporan identity involves the meaning of experience. It seeks to understand the experience and concerns the forma-tion of an identity; a new identity forged out of the diasporan experience. It seeks to provide an existential answer to the question of the meaning of life in the particular place in the 'here and now'. Diaspora is not just about historical forces having a free play with human lives, where the diaspora comes into being through the fortuitous act of nature. While the historians and social philosophers seek to define the nature of diaspora, it is the task of the theologian to interpret its meaning. How then, is the Caribbean diaspora under-stood within Black theological discourse?

The formation of identity

Origin

Three factors constitute the formation of the pan-Caribbean identity. One factor is origin which consists of two sources. These are the pre-existing and the organic. The pre-existing tradition teaches that Caribbean people brought their iden-tity with them to the host country and that it is different from other diasporan identities as well as from that of the Black identity of the host country. Representing this perspective is the Harvard sociologist, Mary Waters. In her book, *West Indian Identities*, she writes that 'black immigrants from the Caribbean come to the United States with a particular identity/culture/worldview that reflects their own unique history and culture'.[20] In demonstrating the distinctiveness of this Caribbean diasporan identity, Waters is careful to observe its history and experience:

> This culture and identity are different from the immigrant identity and culture of previous waves of European immigrants because of their unique history of origin and because of the changed contexts of reception the immigrants face in the United States. This culture and identity are also different from the culture of African Americans.[21]

The contention of this tradition of thought is helpful, in that it enables us to understand that Caribbean people did not arrive in the host country searching for self-understanding but that they came with their own notions intact. This, according to Mary Waters, consists of a moral value of the hard-work ethic, education, monetary investment for the future and preconceived notions of the nature of racial relationships in the host country.[22] For Waters, however, economic success is the purpose of the existence of the Caribbean diaspora. While, economic success is part of the purpose of the diasporic journey, which social scientist Ransford Palmer describes in his seminal work, *The Search for a Better Life*, this is not the sole or even the central purpose. By focusing on the economic dimension of the Caribbean diaspora, Waters ignores the formation of the community that has emerged out of the Caribbean diasporan experience.

The other source of origin is the organic. In contrast to the preformed identity tradition, this tradition proposes the belief that the formation of the pan-Caribbean identity is formed out of the diasporan experience. A major exponent of this tradition is the Caribbean sociologist at the University of Virginia, Milton Vickerman, whose representative work, *Crosscurrent*, provides a useful examination of the emergence of the pan-Caribbean diasporan identity. He takes a social constructivist perspective in defining ethnicity and delineating its understanding in the Caribbean using Jamaica as the representative model because of its population size providing the largest of the Caribbean diasporan communities and because of the other Caribbean nations' sense of identity with Jamaica.[23]

The formation of identity emerges out of the common experience of living in a diaspora, the interaction with other people and combination of social and civic events and involvements along with the systemic constraints of racial discrimination and anti-immigrants hostilities. The persistent practice of alienation, displacement and existential realities of ambivalences and contradictions of diasporan life erode any differences to form a new common identity.[24] What this indicates is that the pan-Caribbean identity is the product of a combination of factors including, history, culture, experience, race and nationality within a particular context. Vickerman offers this insightful observation:

> It takes settlement in metropolitan centers such as London and New York City to form this sense of ethnicity. In these and other cities abroad, Anglophone West Indians confront the difficulties of adjusting to new societies, as manifested in such factors as dealing with regularly with people of another nationalities, obtaining employment and finding places to live.[25]

He further shows that Caribbean people, 'through a combination of social interaction – such as Labor Day Carnival – and deliberate political mobilization, have striven to create a distinct sense of themselves as West Indians?'[26]

As a social construction, Caribbean diasporan identity begins its formation on arrival in the host country. Defining themselves as Black, for example, was not an issue until the beginning of their diasporan journey. They came from a society where race has a different meaning from that which it has, for example, in the United States. Vickerman argues that

'Given this reality, the fact that . . . West Indians would claim to have discovered their "Blackness" only after migrating to America appears puzzling, but only until it is realized that they were referring to the social meanings attributed to skin color, rather than to skin color itself.'[27] In the Caribbean, Vickerman argues, class rather than race defines identity, which engenders the ideology of non-racialism.[28] It is, therefore, normative for Blacks, who constitute the majority of the population to be positions of power and authority. Nevertheless, this so-called Black majority rule, does not bring with it the control of the society's wealth, as David Baronov and Kevin A. Yelvington have argued:

> The Afro-Caribbean population clearly represents the largest ethnic racial group in the Caribbean. At the same time, though Afro-Caribbean people's have achieved political power and many countries, they remain notably lacking among the region's social and economic elites. Thus, despite their declining numbers – as a percentage of the population – and dwindling political clout since the abolition of slavery, Caribbean whites continue to exert disproportional social and economic influence. This is in large measure due to the enormous concentration of wealth and resources in the territories still under their control.[29]

Both the preformed and the organic traditions affirm a pan-Caribbean consciousness and identity. Political scientist, Reuel Rogers, in a provocative essay, 'Black Like Who' argues that the people of the Caribbean diaspora identify themselves according to their national origin and see no contradiction between ethnicity and race. Rogers has made the observation of the existence of the 'exit option'. The 'exit option' advocates the belief that if and when life does not work out as planned, one can return any time to the homeland.[30] Implicit in this option is a sense of uncertainty, unsettledness, alienation in the resident home. This approach, while a viable option, fosters a dual identity but like the preformed identity theory, it does not engender the sense of identity endemic to the Caribbean diasporan existence and essential to the sustenance of the emerging community.

Grounding with the brethren

An important aspect of the formation of the Caribbean diasporan community is the relationship between Caribbean peoples and African-Americans. Vickerman posits the view that Caribbean peoples do not identify themselves as African-Americans. The reasons are many but primarily because of the society's derogatory notion of Blackness. Vickerman writes:

> Basically, West Indian's relationship with African Americans revolves around the process of distancing and identification, sometimes leading to a synthesis of the two . . . They want to be viewed by the society as 'West Indians', an identity which encompasses pride in African ancestry and a focus on achievement.'[31]

There is a reverse side to this self-understanding and attitude that Vickerman observes. He notes 'On a negative note, this attempt at identity construction sometimes involves the holding of negative stereotypes of African American.'[32] Consequently, the Caribbean peoples employ three forms of relating to the African-American consisting of social distancing, racial solidarity and moral exemplar.[33]

This observation is very insightful but it is one-sided. It describes the attitude of Caribbean people towards African-Americans, but what about the converse? It would be interesting to note how African-Americans relate to Caribbean peoples. Vickerman's observation implies the lack of mutuality in the relationship. In fact, the issue should not centre around how Caribbean peoples relate to African-Americans and vice-versa but the interrelationship between both peoples.

While the relationship between Caribbean peoples and

African-Americans is tenuous, the common destiny, in fact, an interwoven destiny, as the meaning of the 'Black experience' indicates, even warrants that more value be given to the forging of an interrelationship or a pan-Black identity of which the pan-Caribbean identity is a species. In reality, the society does not make any distinction among Blacks as the pan-Caribbean identity purports. The African-American philosopher and public intellectual, Cornel West, gave the following account while a professor at Princeton University, in New Jersey.

I left my car – a rather elegant one – in a safe parking lot and stood on the corner of 60th Street and Park Avenue to catch a taxi . . . I waited and waited and waited. After the ninth taxi refused me, my blood began to boil. The tenth taxi refused me and stopped for a kind, well-dressed, smiling, fellow female citizen of European descent. As she stepped in the cab, she said, 'this is really ridiculous, is it not?'

Ugly racial memories of the past flashed through my mind. Years ago, while driving from New York to teach at Williams College, I was stopped on fake charges of trafficking cocaine. When I told the police officer I was a professor of religion, he replied, 'Yeh, and I'm a flying Nun. Let's go nigger!' I was stopped three times in my first ten days in Princeton for driving too slowly on a residential street with speed limit of twenty-five miles per hour.[34]

In principle, ethnicity is the basis of a pan-Caribbean identity but in practice, race is the reality. As far as a pan-Caribbean identity is concerned, it precludes Blackness and adopts the attitude of non-Blacks towards fellow Blacks. Writing of this practice, Mary Waters observes that all other people groups aspire to be White and do not want to be regarded as Blacks. She reports the society's perception and attitude towards Asian and European immigrants and implicitly it includes diasporan people:

In the nineteenth century Irish immigrants were regarded as 'niggers turn inside out' and Negroes were referred to as 'smoked Irish.' Yet over time, the category absorbed these European groups by identifying them as 'not Blacks'. By consciously and assiduously distancing themselves from black Americans these groups became white.[35]

The truth is that racism is a reality of the Caribbean diasporan experience. How they deal with it is a matter of great significance which we will now consider.

Encountering racism

The experience of racism is also a factor in the formation of the pan-Caribbean identity. Racism, Vickerman agues, is a new experience for the Caribbean diasporan community. After discussing the ubiquity of racism in the resident society and its adverse effects on Caribbean diaspora people, he observes the creative means used in response and the emergence of a pan-Caribbean racial awareness. As noted earlier, Caribbean people have been indoctrinated to de-emphasize the seriousness of racism. In explaining this wake-up call to the reality of racism, Vickerman states that 'Because West Indians' prior notions of, and experience with, racial discrimination differ substantially from those prevailing in this country, they experience persistent difficulty dealing with this explicit racism.'[36]

While Vickerman correctly affirms the difference between homeland and resident home racism, he de-emphasizes the nature of it in the homeland. This in no way minimizes the harsh reality of its existence in the resident home. Recognizing this reality in their book, *Inside Babylon: The Caribbean Diaspora in Britain*, Winston James and Clive Harris write:

As to be expected, the harsh realities and perennial winter of British racism, in a number of respects, helped to create an identity – which perhaps under different circumstances would not have developed – among Afro-Caribbeans living in Britain which is more commensurate with their concrete situation and historical experience.[37]

These writers further add that 'the whole experience of living in a White racist society has helped to forge a Black identity where in many cases such an identity did not exist previously or was not consciously thought about'.[38] Racism, therefore, is not a new reality for Caribbean people because they came out of a racist culture.[39]

It is an understatement that racism forms the fabric of Caribbean society. Through slavery and its offspring, colonialism, racism was not only instituted but actively perpetrated. The Caribbean society was based on race where those who were not Whites were regarded as inferior but particularly those who were far removed from any resemblance of having a white pigmentation. The accepted ideology and norm was that the Black person was the absolute lowest member of the human family. Based on the degree of one's pigmentation, a system described as, 'pigmentocracy',[40] otherwise know as 'colorism'[41] as well as 'skinocracy'[42] was developed. This is the ideology that those who have the closest resemblance to being White, which means physical European features such as having a straight nose, long hair and clear skin, are regarded as superior to being Black, while those whose physical characteristics are different, are treated as low class.

The African-American Womanist theologian, Emile Townes, writing about Black identity and colour describes colourism as the interiorized colour consciousness that draws out the various shades of complexion among Black folk, hair texture, and physical features. Colourism is a colour grading that ranges from virtually white to brown to black.[43]

The Caribbean theologian, Kortright Davis concurs and further describes it as an 'elite skinocracy'. It is this notion that persons of 'mixed or Negro race who possess Caucasian characteristics are assured of special attention solely on the basis of their physical appearance ... People with darker skin have traditionally been accorded lower status than people with lighter skin . . .'[44]

The existence and practice of this evil and dehumanizing ideology created double standards as well as a way of life that shapes the identity of the victims, namely, the people of African descent. According to James and Harris, 'In British Caribbean (with the sole exception of Barbados), one was designated legally white after the category of mustee [a mustee is a child of a pure amerindian and a white man] and became automatically free.'[45]

Although the experience of racism is not new to the people of the Caribbean diaspora, they encounter it in a new way in their resident homeland and this experience helps to form their identity. Coming to terms with racism as an integral element in the society, the Caribbean diaspora devises mechanisms to respond. This is done only subsequent to learning of the different understandings of race, the brutality of racism and the resultant formation of a new racial consciousness.[46] Vickerman suggests the use of four methods consisting of confrontation, assertion, resignation and pragmatism as responses or coping strategies.[47] What this suggests is a new and different racial awareness in the Caribbean diaspora. Describing this development, Vickerman writes:

> Over time, continued exposure to racial discrimination causes many West Indians to shift their paradigm from a non-racial one to one that is more explicitly racial. By this, one means that West Indians: (1) come to understand that race permeates all facets of American life; (2) expect to have unpleasant encounters because of race; and (3) often become pessimistic that the United States will become color blind any time soon.[48]

What does this say about the formation of a pan-Caribbean identity? It could be understood as opportunistic where one is only seeking his or her own survival without regard for the welfare of others. It promotes a survivalist rather than an emancipatory purpose. Furthermore, it employs an accommodationist strategy, which, while it benefits particular individuals, does not address the causes and issues of the structural and systemic practices that militate against its own existence such as the reason for migration and the perpetration of racial injustice, economic exploitation, political oppression and social and cultural degradation. In other words, the pan-Caribbean identity is far too provincial and parochial. It has not connected the particular struggle of the Caribbean diaspora to the larger struggle of Black people. It is important to analyse the particular situation but not apart from the general situation and the intent to obtain the emancipation of all Black people.

These are some of the realities facing the pan-Caribbean identity, but there are two fundamental issues, the seeking of the common and affirming of a common heritage, that are missing in the formation of this identity.

The missing links

What has emerged from this study of the formation of a distinct Caribbean diasporan community is the centrality of ethnicity. The emphasis, however, on individual achievements, denies the moral virtue of the common good in the Caribbean religious tradition, decentralizes Caribbean history and heritage and excludes the centrality of the Christian faith in Caribbean diasporan culture. I will, therefore, seek to affirm the value of the common good, and assert the significance of Caribbean heritage as missing ingredients in the pan-Caribbean identity.

The common good

The Caribbean diaspora's emphasis on individual achievements fosters individualism which violates a cardinal value in Caribbean religious tradition. Individual achievement,

Vickermann argues, is the goal of the pan-Caribbean identity. He states: 'These immigrants perceive themselves as sober, hard-working individuals who possess definite goals and are willing to sacrifice to achieve it.'[49] The Caribbean religious tradition encourages these practices and regards them as virtues to be cultivated not as ends in themselves but for the interest of the common good which is the foremost goal of the life of faith. Writing about the centrality of the common good in Black spirituality, the African-American social ethicist, Peter Paris in his *The Spirituality of African Peoples*, observes: 'African peoples agree that . . . ethnic community is the paramount social reality apart from which humanity cannot exist . . . community is a sacred phenomenon created by the supreme God, protected by the divinities and governed by the ancestral spirits.'[50] The individual is important to the community but she is not primary. The idea of the primacy of the individual is alien to Caribbean religious tradition. This does not mean that the tradition does not value individual conscience and liberty and responsibility. It does, but it is within the context of the community that the individual derives these rights and responsibilities. A distinction, however, must be made between individuality and individualism. Making this distinction, Cornel West in his valuable book, *Prophecy Deliverance: An Afro-American Revolutionary Christianity*, writes:

> The norm of individuality reinforces the importance of community, the common good and the harmonious development of personality. And it stands in stark contrast to those doctrinaire individualisms which promote human selfishness, denigrate the idea of community, and distort the holistic development of personality. The norm of individuality conceives persons as enjoyers and agents of their uniquely human capacities, whereas the norm of doctrinaire individualism views them as maximizers of pleasure and appropriators of unlimited resources.[51]

Individualism, also, alters the relationship between the individual and the community. The quest for emancipation reflects the spiritual and moral yearnings and belief of Black people as observed in the various emancipatory movements from the period of slavery through the time of colonialism to the present era. This is also the case in the formation of the Caribbean diaspora community. The individual-centred orientation, however, does not ground nor relate to this self-understanding of the quest for emancipation nor provide any analysis of the Black condition, especially the migration movement. Writing of the relationship between the individual and the community, Peter Paris provides an instructive observation:

> Consonant with their understanding of their African forebears, [Black] African Americans have always known that persons cannot flourish apart from a community of belonging. They have also known that any community that oppresses its members is not community at all but, rather, a seething cauldron of dissension, distrust, and bitterness. Thus they have no difficulty in discerning a moral contradiction at the heart of the American republic: a contradiction caused by the primacy of racism as the organizing principle in the nation's public life. . . . They have never been able to conceive of society structures or their leaders as morally neutral in the exercise of their duties. Nor . . . view their resistance to racism in anything other than moral terms.[52]

The existence as a diasporan community warrants that they know and act as one community in order to rid society of its unjust and systemic oppressive policies and structures. Individual well-being is integrally related to the one struggle for emancipation. As a diasporan community that is not only marginal but a minority in the society, it is essential that the Caribbean diaspora realize that individual and communal survival depends on the commitment and willingness to work together.[53] In this regard, it becomes necessary to examine the all-important issue of Caribbean history and heritage in the formation of the Caribbean diasporan community.

Common history and heritage

The history and heritage of the Caribbean diaspora is an integral element in the formation of a pan-Caribbean identity which has not been taken into account by the ethnicity identity theory. The experience of living in a foreign country is one of displacement, alienation and hostility. When, however, there is the opportunity to discover and become involved with persons and community of a common heritage and history, there is a liberating sense of affinity and identity. In his classic novel, *Lonely Londonders*, the Trinidadian writer, Sam Selvon, writing about the life of Caribbean people in the British diaspora of the mid-twentieth century, describes this experience in the following account:

> In the grimness of the winter, with your hand plying space like a blind man's stick in the yellow fog, with ice on the ground and a coldness defying effort to keep warm, the boys coming and going, working, eating, sleeping, going about the vast metropolis like veteran Londoners.
> Nearly every Sunday morning, like if they going to church, the boys lining in Moses room, coming together for a old talk, to find out the latest gen, what happening, when is the next fete. Bart asking if anybody see his girl anywhere, Cap recounting an episode he had with a woman by the tube station the night before, Big City want to know why the arse he can't win a pool, Galahad recounting a clash with the color problem in a restaurant in Piccadilly, Harris saying he hope the weather turns, Five saying he have to drive a truck to Glasgow tomorrow.[54]

What this account raises are not only issues of the emergence and formation of a community, the incessant need for relationships, the brutal existential realities of race, class and the hardships of life but the merging of nationalities, cultures and experiences to formulate a distinct identity. It is also important to observe that this description of diasporan existence is the recognition and affirmation of Caribbean history and heritage which form the core of the Caribbean diasporan self-understanding. Winston James and Clive Harris, who correctly acknowledge this essentiality, state:

> [T]here has thus been a pan-Caribbeanization of the cultures of those from individual countries and territories of the region. Languages, idioms, cuisines, music and so on, have scaled their individual boundaries and have become far more generalized, shared and amalgamated within the Caribbean diaspora than within the Caribbean itself.[55]

Advancing this understanding, the Jamaican historian and public intellectual, Rex Nettleford, writing about the Caribbean heritage argues that

> this is severance from ancestral home whether it's from Africa, Europe, Lebanon, India, China, or the indigenous Caribbean itself originally inhabited by Arawaks and Caribs. It constitutes suffering under enslavement, indentureship, and colonialism. It also constitutes *survival* and what exists beyond that survival . . .[56]

Nettleford's contention is that the elements of the severance from ancestral heritage, the experience of sufferings and acts of survival are what constitute the Caribbean heritage and form the source and the foundation for building a pan-Caribbean identity. James and Harris observe this phenomenon and describe it as a nascent pan-Caribbeanism which started to emerge in the Caribbean migration movement to Europe and North America.[57] They ground their view on the Barbadian writer, George Lamming's, novel of 1954, *The Emigrant*, in which he articulates this emerging pan-Caribbeanism.

It is here that one sees a discovery actually taking shape. No Barbadian, no Trinidadian, no St. Lucian, no islander from the West Indies himself is a West Indian until he encounters another islander in a foreign territory. It was only when the Barbadian childhood corresponded with the Grenadian or the Guinanese childhood in important details of folk-lore, that the wider identification was arrived at.[58]

Grounding identity

The pan-Caribbean identity, however, includes more than the virtue of the common good and value of its history and heritage. These do not adequately define the identity without the centrality of faith. In seeking to discover a pan-Caribbean self-understanding, the diasporan experience is to be examined theologically. A theological interpretation is an examination of identity and the diasporan experience in light of the Christian faith premised on Jesus Christ as the emancipator of all humanity as expressed by the gospel of Luke:

> The Spirit of the Lord is upon me, because he has anointed me to bring good news to the poor. He has sent me to proclaim release to the captives and recovery of sight to the blind, to let the oppressed go free, to proclaim the year of the Lord's favor. (Luke 4.18–19)

Faith in Jesus Christ is the single most important element in the existence and survival of the Caribbean people. It continues to play such a role in the sustenance of the diaspora. The Caribbean/African-American Dialogue and the Caribbean Conference of Churches states in their 'Verdun Proclamation' of 1992 that

> The one factor which allowed the peoples of the Caribbean to survive was their belief systems or religion. These religious beliefs and practices gave these people, especially

the African population the fortitude they needed to with-
stand the dehumanizing practices of the Europeans.[59]

The African philosopher of religion, John Mbiti says it
brilliantly:

> To be human is to belong to the whole community, and to
> do so involves participating in the beliefs, ceremonies, and
> rituals and festivals of that community. A person cannot
> detach himself from the religion of his group, for to do
> so is to be severed from his roots, his foundation, his
> context of security, his kinships and the entire group of
> those who made him aware of his own existence. To be
> without one of these corporate is be out of the whole
> picture. Therefore, to be without religion amounts to a
> self-excommunication from the entire life of the society,
> and African peoples do not know how to exist without
> religion.[60]

The issue, however, is not about the contents of faith as an
objective body of belief or the nature of faith as a subjective
act but an interpretation of the diasporan self-understanding
and experience in light of this faith that the doctrines of the
incarnation of Jesus Christ and the event of Pentecost
express.

The incarnation of Jesus Christ

In contrast to a social constructionist understanding of identity, a theological interpretation of the pan-Caribbean identity is faith-based. One of the two principles of faith is the
incarnation of Jesus Christ. The incarnation is an act of the
sovereignty of God and a gift from God. Without denying
the active involvement of human beings in the formation of
an identity, the contention is that ethnicity is the context,
ingredient and means that expresses the particularity of an
identity. It takes into consideration the particular, consisting

of the totality of social and existential situation, race, class, gender, nationality, place and all that constitute the nature of life in a particular context. The incarnation of Jesus Christ,[61] for example, takes place in a particular person, at a particular place and time but most significantly, it is also an act initiated by God. The Christian Scriptures state:

> In the Beginning was the Word, and the Word was with God and the Word was God. He was in the beginning with God . . . And the Word became flesh and lived among us, and we have seen his glory, the glory as of a father's only son, full of grace and truth. (John 1.1—2.14)

This raises two issues for the study. One is that God acted on God's own accord. God took the initiative to enter human history. St Paul writes: 'But God proves his love for us in that while we still were sinners Christ died for us' (Rom. 5.8). The second is that Jesus was a particular human being. He had a particular gender, nationality and ethnicity. This to say he was male, Jewish and Black.[62]

Above all, the incarnation is a diasporan act. It involves movement, exile, longing for home and formation of identity as diaspora indicates. It is a movement, even dispersal from eternal existence to earthly existence and also a change in identity from divine to human as Paul argued in what theologians define as the *kenosis*. In expressing this understanding of God becoming human in Jesus Christ, Paul writes:

> Who, though he was in the form of God, did not regard equality with God as something to be exploited, but emptied himself taking the form of a slave, being born in human likeness. And being found in human form, he humbled himself and became obedient to the point of death – even death on a cross. (Phil. 2.6–8)

The prophetic writings further describe this diasporan experience. These writings acknowledge Jesus as Emmanuel, which means 'God with us'. 'Therefore the Lord himself shall give you a sign . . . ' according to the prophet Isaiah, 'and shall name him Immanuel' (Isa. 7.14; NSRV). The Christian Scripture identifies this person as Jesus. According to the 'birth narratives',

> Now the birth of Jesus the Messiah took place in this way . . . All this took place to fulfil what had been spoken by the Lord through the prophet: 'Look, the virgin shall conceive and bear a son, and they will name him Emmanuel, which means "God is with us".' (Matt. 1.18, 22–23)

There are other instances that illustrate the incarnation of Jesus Christ as a diasporan person. The biblical record states he migrated to Egypt. In giving his account of this significant event, which the gospel writer interprets as divine initiative, he states: 'Now after they had left, an angel of the Lord appeared to Joseph in a dream and said. "Get up, take the child and his mother and flee to Egypt . . ."' (Matt. 2.13). After a period of time, he journeyed from Egypt back to Israel where he lived in the country town of Nazareth. Similar to the decision to migrate to Egypt as a divine initiative, emigrating from Egypt was also one of divine initiative. 'When Herod died, an angel of the Lord suddenly appeared in a dream to Joseph in Egypt and said, "Get up, take the child and his mother and go to the land of Israel"' (Matt. 2.19ff.). The incarnation, therefore, is an essential component of the theological basis and framework within which Caribbean diasporan Christians not only ground their faith but interpret the diasporan experience. In this experience, the emancipatory purpose and event of Christ takes root in the particularities of their humanity which, in this context, is the Caribbean diasporan ethnicity.

The event of Pentecost

The event of the day of Pentecost is another principle of faith on which a pan-Caribbean identity is based. Pentecost was originally a Jewish harvest festival known as the Feast of Weeks. It took place at the end of their harvest when they brought their offerings of bread and animals as expressions of gratitude to God according to their religious laws (Exod. 25.16; Lev. 23.15–21; Num. 28.26; Deut. 16.9–12). Following the destruction of the first temple in 586 BC, this festival eventually developed into a celebration of the giving of the Law which reveals God's character and will and leads to a covenantal relationship with God.[63] In the Christian tradition, this is a revelation of God through the Holy Spirit based on Jesus Christ and through faith in him leads to the formation of a new community as God's people.

In the first place, like the incarnation of Jesus Christ, the event of Pentecost is a gift from God. Luke expresses this perspective in the answer he gave in response to the question of the meaning of Pentecost (Acts 2.14–21; Joel 2.28–32). Interestingly, this is similar to the New Testament understanding of salvation. According to the apostle Paul:

> But God, who is rich in mercy, out of the great love with which he loved us even when we were dead through our trespasses made us alive in Christ – by grace you have been saved . . . through faith – and this is not your own doing, it is the gift of God . . . (Eph. 2.4–10; Gal. 4.26–29)

God gave this gift on the day of Pentecost which is believed to be the historical birth of the Church, constituted by people of diverse origins,[64] similar to the nature of the Caribbean diasporan community.

In the second place, again like the incarnation, the event of Pentecost is a diasporan act. Pentecost was a celebrative gathering of the Jewish diaspora in Jerusalem. The Jewish people were dispersed throughout the Roman Empire. Each year they assembled in Jerusalem to celebrate their faith. On the day of Pentecost, the Spirit that breathed life to create the universe is the same Spirit that breathed life to create the Church. Giving an account of this act, Luke reports:

> When the day of Pentecost had come, they were all together in one place. And suddenly from heaven there came a sound like the rush of a violent wind, and it filled the entire house where they were sitting . . . All of them were filled with the Holy Spirit . . . Now there were devout Jews from every nation under heaven living in Jerusalem . . . (Acts. 2.1ff.)

As this newly formed community of Christ's followers grew and became a distinct community of faith, it got a new identity. It was described as a commonwealth (Eph. 2.12), race, nation and people (1 Pet. 2.9–10). The idea of a distinct identity finds ultimate expression in the eschatological vision of their nature and destiny. The writer of Revelation gives the following account: 'After this I looked, and there was a great multitude that no one could count, from every nation, and from all tribes and peoples and languages standing before the throne and before the Lamb . . .' (Rev. 7.9ff.). This account is a testimony of the diversity of biblical faith. It is diversity not only by the social locations but also in ethnicities, nationalities and races and cultures.[65] As indicated through the Pentecost event, the Spirit of God sets in motion an explosion of the creation of new and distinct communities of faith.

The Caribbean diasporan church is an expression of this creation. It too grows and becomes a distinct community of faith made out of a diverse people. What has emerged, in this distinct community, is no less or more than what God has done in history through the incarnation of Jesus Christ and the event of Pentecost. In fact, the maxim 'all o' we is one'[66] the Caribbeanization of Jamaica's motto, 'Out of many, one people'[67] and the guiding philosophy of Marcus Garvey's

United Negro Improvement Association, 'One God! One Aim! One Destiny!'[68] are attestations to this belief and self-understanding. These expressions, in addition, underscore and inform the quest to forge communal existence out of the crucible of diasporan experience.

Furthermore, the Spirit that created the biblical community of faith is the same Spirit at work in the creation of the Caribbean diasporan church. The biblical testimony affirms this act (Acts 15.7–11). The Spirit works not only to create community but in the ministry of individuals. Consider, for example, Paul's case against the Galatians, which was not about diversity but the ministerial authority. The Galatian Christians questioned Paul's ministerial authority. He informed them by affirming that the Spirit that was working in the 'super-apostles' is the same Spirit working in his ministry. He states: 'For God who worked through Peter making him an apostle to the circumcised also worked through me in sending me to the Gentiles' (Gal. 2.8). Thus, we can conclude that the understanding of faith in a Caribbean diasporan theology is that the Spirit that created the biblical communities of faith and worked in the life and ministry of these people is the same Spirit working in the creation of the Caribbean diasporan church.

Conclusion

The formation of a Caribbean diaspora as a distinct community is a difficult and complex issue. We are confronted with the reality of a growing population of people of diverse heritage, nationalities and race but of a common history. This diversity warrants the construction of a Caribbean identity knowing that the Black community is not monolithic but diverse and no single Black people group is, nor represents, the whole Black diaspora. This poses two challenges. On the one hand, it is to ensure that it does not separate itself from the family of Black people and consequently create a form of separatism. On the other hand, it is to affirm the particularity of ethnicity and the peculiarity of faith without asserting assimilation into the majority culture. This is an issue of knowing how to remain Caribbean while being diasporan.

These challenges are being met as this study indicates with the Christian faith as its centre and God's emancipatory purpose in Jesus Christ as the framework that defines and interprets the meaning of identity and community. It is in this regard that the theorists of ethnicity are to consider the significance of faith in the diasporan experience in order to understand the emancipatory purpose of God in the formation of identity, community and peoplehood.

8. The Nature of Homophobia in the Black Church

CAROLINE REDFEARN

Preamble

This chapter is part of a larger research project, whose working title is 'The Nature of Homophobia in the Black Church and the Movement towards Inclusivity'. My funding submission was drafted in the context of a call to ministry while I was a member of the Assembly of God Church, when living and working in the Caribbean (Jamaica and the Cayman Islands) from 1982 to 1997. I am pursuing an inclusive ministry that offers spiritual support and guidance to people of African-Caribbean descent, their friends and families of all gender identities and sexual orientations. This includes people who are largely excluded and demonized by many churches and Christian groups; people who are within minority categories relating to gender identities and roles (intersex or hermaphrodites and transpeople, etc.) and those with other sexual orientations (homosexuals, lesbians, bisexuals, etc.).

The purpose of my research is twofold:

1 To enable people of African-Caribbean descent and mixed parentage, who have diverse sexual identities and orientations, to find value and meaning in a culturally relevant, 'inclusive' Black theology for the UK.
2 To empower a conscious Black church to have cultural and historical reference points that provide a basis for developing a theology that speaks to the needs of sexual

minorities and newer patterns of domestic relationships within the African-Caribbean community in Britain.

This chapter has a clearly defined focus and objective: to consider possible historical underpinnings to homophobia.[1] I am therefore excluding traditional biblical interpretation as this will be addressed on another occasion.

Background – definitions

On completing my funding application I was acutely aware of my lack of forethought in my use of the term 'homophobia' – did I meant heterodoxy or heterosexism or even hetero-centrism? Similarly how does one define homosexuality or homosexualities as distinct from homoeroticism, homo-socialities, homoemotionalities or homosensualities? Did my term include phobias towards lesbians and consider biphobia and transphobia?

Definitions of homophobia

Cassell's Queer Companion defines homophobia as

the fear or hatred of homosexuals and is colloquially used as the word for beliefs which explicitly or implicitly denigrate lesbians and gay men. Matters such as verbal assaults, physical attacks, the removal of the children of lesbian and gay parents, and discrimination in housing, employment, tax, pensions and immigration are all commonly ascribed to homophobia.[2]

Kelly Brown Douglas states: 'Homophobia refers to the oppressive and bigoted attitudes and behaviours that black people, as well as others, often direct toward gay and lesbian persons.'[3] There are those who object to the term as Cooper writes in *Sound Clash*.

In Jamaica, homosexuality is routinely denounced because
it is perceived as a marker of difference from the sexual/
cultural 'norm'. Further, many Jamaicans vigorously object
to being labelled as 'homophobic'. Claiming their heterosexuality as 'normative' they reject the negative connotations of the 'phobia' in homophobia. For them it is
homosexuality that is the morbidity – not their culturally
legitimated aversion to it.[4]

A definition of heterosexism

Others prefer the term heterosexism 'as a way of distancing
. . . from the reactionary implications of the term homophobia' . . . [which] 'implies that anti-gay and lesbian talk or
actions are a result of individual pathology, rather than
something embedded in existing social relations and practices that we all need to address'.[5]

Kelly Brown Douglas intimates that 'heterosexism signals
the complex systems and structures that privilege heterosexual orientations, whilst explicitly or implicitly penalizing
same-sexed orientations'.[6] Others like Farajaje-Jones, 'an
avowed gay-identified, bisexual Black theologian' uses the
term 'heterosexism' to mean 'the systematic display of homo-
phobia/biphobia in the institutions of society: they work
together to reinforce compulsory heterosexuality and the
nuclear family'.[7]

Definitions of homosexuality

In defining homosexuality, much can be said of the social
construction of sexual identities, in particular, the historical
movement from a single sexual act to what Clark refers to as
the invention of homosexuality 'as a permanent personality
state'.

The term [homosexual] first appeared in an 1869 pam-
phlet by the Hungarian Karoly Maria Kertbeny which put

a case for the repeal of Prussia's anti-gay legislation. It initially caught on among scientific and academic publications, and gained widespread currency in the early twentieth century.[8]

Other authors, notably John Boswell, have deposed the term 'homosexual' as adjectival with a preference for the term 'gay' which refers to persons who are 'conscious of an erotic inclination toward their own gender as a distinguishing characteristic or, loosely, to things associated with such people'.[9] This, in turn, has been superseded by the reinvention of the term 'queer' that rose to prominence in the 1990s.

It was a reaction to narrow identity politics, rigid categories and separate groups that had come to characterize the movement. With Queer Politics all identities – lesbian, gay, bisexual, transsexual, even some heterosexual – could merge into a general 'queerness' . . . but unlike the non-threatening civil rights agendas of the past gay and lesbian movement . . . the queer approach was critical and oppositional.[10]

Farajaje-Jones provides a diasporan perspective, removed from Western essentialism that standardizes and markets 'gay' identity and culture as white and middle class. He writes '(w)e have a much more fluid spectrum of sexualities than does the white community'.[11] He uses the term '"in-the-life" because it has been used in [our] African-American tradition for generations to connote a broad spectrum of identities and behaviours and because of the rich spiritual connotations of the word "life" especially for a people continually confronted with suffering and death.'[12] In reference to homosexualities and bisexualities, he speaks of

homosocialities (the phenomenon of people in various cultures, institutions or situations spending a significant part of their time and life-experience exclusively in the presence

of people of their own gender group) and homosensualities (physical contact, or the exchange of physical affec-
tion, such as holding hands or kissing, between people of
the same gender, which is non-genitocentric and non-
orgasmocentric).[13]

Another term that requires some thought is that of homoeroticism – often defined as 'all erotic-sexual encounters and
experiences of people with persons of the same sex, whether
the person is considered homosexual or not'.[14] Finally, in
succinct Jamaica talk – as Cooper writes there is the term
'battyman . . . encodes anal sex'.[15]

Incidentally, as an aside, Nissinen in his historical analysis
of homoeroticism in the biblical world discusses the term
'abomination' which implies homoerotic behaviour associated with 'cultic practices'[16] of which child sacrifice is one.

Buggery/sodomy or homosexuality/homosexualities?

To what sexual phenomena am I alluding in this research?
Am I speaking of buggery/sodomy or homosexuality/homo-
sexualities? Betteridge, in his preface to the analysis of
sodomy in early modern Europe, has observed that many
'gay historiographers'[17] in their discussions on sodomy, have
challenged the use of the modern term 'homosexuality' to
describe past events in early modern Europe. Salih, in her
extract on sexual identities operating within a medieval
framework, makes the interesting observation that

> while premodern sexuality may be envisaged as consisting
> of a number of more or less transgressive acts, modern
> sexuality is claimed to be organised into identity categories
> which are saturated with meaning; whom a person desires
> can be assumed also to imply other details of their person-
> alities and preferences.[18]

She acknowledges that 'medieval terms like "sodomy" . . .

fluctuate and may include any non-reproductive sexual act, as well as sins which are not sexual at all'.[19] She challenges 'medievalists' to consider a continuum of sexual identities. Jordon, goes further and posits the notion that 'sodomy was invented by medieval theologians' as there was 'no trace of the term before the eleventh century'.[20]

Other historians deliberately use the term 'sodomy' because it 'fits more comfortably in a seventeenth century context than homosexuality . . . and the layered academic or cultural definitions'[21] are absent. While acknowledging that in Tudor and Stuart England, 'sodomy' and 'buggery' were interchangeable, he notes that

> (a)t various times sodomy and buggery, as defined by law, included homosexual acts, homosexual child molestation (but never heterosexual child molestation), bestiality, heterosexual anal-genital contact, and assorted methods of homosexual masturbation.[22]

His resulting definition is simple – sodomy refers to 'homosexual contact between adult males'.[23] It is probably prudent to also indicate that sodomy was used to describe 'uncleanness, a general term for deviant sexual behaviour'.

The focus of this chapter

For the purposes of this discussion I am focusing on penetrative (anal) sex between men, consensual or otherwise. It is commonly referred to as buggery or sodomy (a more complex word that I shall return to later) and I am aware that it does feature in heterosexual relationships. Similarly I am conscious that not all men who have sex with men consider themselves to be homosexual: whether 'on the down low'[24] or not. Nor do all homosexual activities involve penetration, that is sodomy.

In *Webster's Dictionary*, buggery is defined by the noun – sodomy, which in turn is defined as 'carnal copulation between male persons or with beasts'. It may be of interest to know that homosexuality is not illegal in Jamaica, but buggery is, which is described in Section 76 of the 'Offences Against the Person Act' as 'anal intercourse with any human being or beast'. A person charged with the offence may be sentenced up to ten years in prison with hard labour. It differs from the Webster definition in that it allows for the prosecution of consenting heterosexual couples and is probably a legacy from colonialism. It was Henry VIII who first 'brought sodomy within the purview of statute law'.[25] Even 'consensual sodomy is illegal'.[26]

This work is undertaken with respect to the Black church in Britain. It is not the place to unpack this term at this juncture, but it is worth noting that I see this term as a very heterogeneous one that incorporates a variety of ecclesiological, denominational, cultural and theological perspectives.[27]

Sexual behaviour and activity during slavery in Jamaica

Historical accounts, analyses, autobiographies and personal journals of slave conditions in the British West Indies contribute significantly to an understanding of the nature of sexual behaviours and relationships on the plantations. While data on heterosexual activity is extensive, there is a dearth of data on other forms of sexual behaviour, with sometimes just the mere suggestion of sodomy as male rape and other possible non-consensual homosexual practices. Similarly, while the study of enslaved women has generated additional investigation, a similar analysis has not been directed towards relationships between Black male slaves themselves or with their White male slave owners and traders, beyond their economic relationship and the demonization of Black male heterosexuality. Perhaps the disparity is due to the recognition that the 'White male master's relationship with Black women slaves was intrinsically more complex than that with male slaves, influenced by gender conflicts, sexual tensions, and his ownership of her unborn children.'[28] In addition, sexual liaisons with White masters accrued benefits to the female slave that were unavailable to Black men, unless perhaps in consensual homosexual activity. Moreover, it is unclear as to whether references to 'aberrant sexual behaviour'[29] in nineteenth-century Cuba, for example, may or may not allude to such practices.

Jamaican society under slavery – White society

The Jamaican slave plantocracy of the eighteenth century was categorized by Patterson as an 'absentee society' through the tendency of its affluent owners to reside in England. His analysis indicates a White expatriate culture deficient in effective civil and political leadership and financial propriety. The unstable and largely illiterate population displayed a high mortality rate with a rapid turnover of new arrivals from England that kept the population in flux, compounded by the near collapse of marriage and family life as stabilizing institutions.

> The absence of the most educated and civilized members of the society also led to a complete breakdown of religion and morality among the resident Whites since the local leaders were among the most profligate people imaginable. What was worse, the clergymen themselves were often among the most immoral in the island and the established Anglican church in Jamaica represents, perhaps the most disgraceful episode in the history of that institution . . . It was well known that unsuccessful overseers with the right contacts could procure a living as a clergyman . . . Holy orders were readily given to men who were imperfectly educated and of an indifferent moral character.[30]

Societal dysfunction was further encouraged by the scarcity of White women, prohibitions on marriage for White employees on some estates (to prevent financial dependants) and socially sanctioned promiscuity and cohabitation. 'It was the greatest disgrace for a White man not to cohabit with some women *or other*[31] quoted one slave owner in the author's analysis. (Note the possible veiled reference to homosexual activity.) The island's degeneration into sexual anarchy is demonstrated in the following extract.

> The sexual exploitation of female slaves by White men was the most disgraceful and iniquitous aspect of Jamaican slave society. Rape and the seduction of infant slaves; the ravishing of the common law wives of the male slaves under the threat of punishments, and the out-right sadism often involving the most heinous forms of sexual torture were the order of the day. [32]

This is corroborated by other authors, including Morrissey, who states:

> Sexual relationships between European males and slaves and the severity with which female slaves were physically abused are not entirely separate phenomena. For some sadistic owners sexuality and punishment were perversely linked.[33]

Dunn, in his study of sugar and slaves in the English West Indies in 1624–1713, graphically illustrated the sadistic tendencies of the planters: 'The seventeenth-century English sugar planters created one of the harshest systems of servitude in Western history.'[34] Punishment of slaves ranged from castration, beheading, being 'drawn and quartered', torn to pieces by dogs, to being roasted alive. This prompted one historian to pass the following indictment: 'In the Caribbean, rebellious slaves were butchered indiscriminately, tortured for confessions and publicly executed in a style which would have been more familiar to Englishmen of the late Middle Ages.'[35]

In this sexually charged and abusive environment, it is highly probable that the sexual brutality of the plantations also included forced and unsolicited homosexual practices, for Patterson's analysis attests to 'the breakdown of *all* forms of social sanctions relating to sexual behaviour'.[36]

Black slave society: sexual relationships and Black sexuality

Walvin concurs, when he states that

> On the plantations White women were scarce for they generally preferred to be absent from rural properties, enjoying instead whatever pleasures and delights were available in the local towns and ports. White men on the plantations, from the planter to the book-keeper, turned to slave women for sexual companionship. Their relationships ranged from the basest of sexual intimidation and violence – against which the slave women had no defence – through to long lasting and monogamous 'marriages'.[37]

Speaking of the sexual depravity of White colonial planters Walvin amplifies his point by recounting the conduct of one Thomas Thistlewood. He writes,

> Few planters could have been as sexually aggressive as Thomas Thistlewood. He took his slaves wherever he found them, in the fields, in the various plantation buildings, but most of all in his own house: in his bedroom, in the hall, kitchen, or on any piece of furniture which was nearby. In his home he ruled supreme, and any woman working there was likely to find herself pressed into sexual service for her master's pleasure . . . Thistlewood seduced slaves by the dozen – each coupling recorded with an attention to detail that defies explanation.[38]

To the repressed European, the openness of African sexuality and in particular that of the women, proved 'provocative' recounts Morrissey. She suggests that the 'act of enslavement and social subjugation may have stimulated the sexual imagination of some highly repressed Europeans'.[39] While acknowledging the currency of sexual relationships with White men as survival strategies for many Black women, she articulates the lurid tapestry of sexual and physical abuse within the plantation system. This includes the narratives alleging excessive cruelty towards Black female slaves by White women. Denied socially sanctioned opportunities for liaisons with Black men, it is alleged their disapproval of sexual miscegenation and their corresponding 'desexualization' fuelled their jealousy and was subsequently manifested in their cruelty. Walvin supports this contention when he writes,

> Long before the development of the American slave empires, Blacks were thought of as particularly lascivious and sexual beings. Blackness, nakedness, lust and immorality; these, in various combinations were stock ingredients of English accounts of Africa and Africans . . . It was assumed that Africans – men and women – were especially lascivious, particularly well-endowed by nature and were propelled by their hot tropical homelands into a realm of sexuality unknown to the Europeans.[40]

Fantasies surrounded Black female sexuality and the West Indies. Jamaica, for example, was presented as 'a land of sexual opportunity for the young European males'.[41] Their preference for young, light-skinned women was noted. Patterson records the proliferation of physical and sexual abuse faced by Black slave women in Jamaica; which included widespread rape on plantations, having been procured by pimps (estate midwives) for enforced prostitution in towns where slave ownership was absent.

Homosexualities

In his later work *Rituals of Blood* Patterson makes the following observation: 'Though we hear only of the rape and sexual abuse of girls, it is hard to believe that slave boys were not raped by homosexual slaveholders.'[42] In his notes I found this interesting addition:

> Steven Brown states that 'in no cases did slaves mention homosexual assaults' in their interviews and narratives, in his 'Sexuality and the Slave Community' . . . this is hardly surprising, since it is only in recent years, with radically different attitudes towards sexual abuse, that men have been able to bring themselves to admit to having been sexually assaulted by older men when they were boys. I have two reasons for speculating that homosexual assaults took place. First, in every known human society, a small minority of men are homosexuals – between 3 and 6 percent – and in the highly probable event that homosexual Euro-Americans found themselves with total power, and no risk of arrest, over fine-looking slave boys, it is a reasonable assumption that they would have exploited them in some cases. If homosexual priests cannot resist the temptation to abuse their authority over boys in their charge, it is hard to see why slave mongers, overseers, and owners would. My second reason is the fact that southern culture was highly honorific, with considerable degrees of male bonding and homoerotic male play. We know from the literature on honorific societies that they tend to have a higher than normal proportion of homosexuals.[43]

A contemporary and collaborative adjunct to this is present in the writings of the Jamaican author, O'Brien Dennis in *The Cries of Men*. In documenting his experience of being sexually abused, the author writes '[t]he hardest part of recovery for me was coming out and admitting that I was sexually abused'.[44] And again:

Sexual abuse has nothing to do with lust, passion or love it's all about power dynamics. When a boy is sexually abused by a man, it is often incorrectly seen as a homosexual act. No single factor is more responsible for the stigma attached to male rape than homophobia, the irrational fear and hatred of homosexuality.[45]

I was aware of the numerous publications on African sexualities that included same-sex relationships. African homosexualities remain a highly contested arena for scholarly discourse. I will be reviewing this literature in the larger research work from which this essay is drawn. Amplifying this point, Griffin states: 'many Afrocentric thinkers have claimed that homosexuality is a perverse sexual practice unknown to Africans until it was imposed on them by Europeans ... Research indicates instead that homosexuality existed in Africa, like the rest of the world, prior to European colonialism.'[46]

In the rest of the world, including the Americas and the Caribbean, Baird notes the discovery of sodomy by the Spanish among the indigenous tribes during the sixteenth century. She cites examples from 1513 of 'sodomites' literally being thrown to the dogs and of the Aztec civilization being 'rife with sodomy'. Most germane to our discussion – 'Elsewhere in the region, Europeans were seeking and finding sodomy. One Spanish conquistador asserted the Caribs "were sodomites more than any other race".'[47]

With reference to English homosexualities, there are volumes of historical data and analyses on the discovery, creation and development of this phenomenon. This I will discuss fully in my doctoral thesis where I will construct a 'Genealogy of Sexualities'. However, it is useful to review precolonial attitudes towards sodomy, homosexuality and sexuality generally within the framework of seventeenth to nineteenth-century thinking that has exerted an impact on contemporary sexualities.

Some have concluded that eighteenth-century England witnessed the beginning of a 'sexual revolution' which transformed attitudes, creating a phallocentric and increasingly heterosexual culture, which saw forms of behaviour beyond the bounds of penetrative heterosexuality as 'unnatural'.[48] In support of his hypothesis, Hitchcock examines commonly held medical views within that century, that Galenic humours (phlegm, blood, and black and yellow biles) controlled human development in combination with environmental factors. In effect 'all people were believed to be on a gradient from male to female characteristics depending on the quantity and quality of humoral life essence possessed by the individual',[49] thus creating a 'one body' representation of sexual differentiation that ensured biological sex was 'a matter of degree, rather than type'. The development towards a 'two body' depiction in the latter part of the century was perceived as indicative of 'a broad social need to redefine women as fundamentally different from men'.[50] Similarly with the development and rise of a medical elite, by the early nineteenth century men and women had been 'effectively redefined . . . as fundamentally and "naturally" different'.[51]

A development parallel within the medical model was the flourishing, London-based 'molly' cultures at the end of the seventeenth and early eighteenth centuries. For many historians, these social gatherings in ale houses and clubs, enabling sex among men, heralded 'the first recognisable homosexual identity'.[52] While sodomy was in some cases associated with heresy and witchcraft, many debate the equation of the practice of buggery with a homosexual lifestyle at that time. It is perceived that anal sex between men was a normal part of sexuality, even for heterosexual males. The rise of the 'molly house' was indicative of 'a well developed and sophisticated homosexual subculture' with 'a well established set of outdoor meeting places distributed throughout London, and that a separate culture of gesture, expression and dress allowed homosexual men to recognize each other and to contexualize their love-making within a sophisticated ritualized formula'.[53]

For many scholars, homosexuality is best understood as a social construct. The creation of safe, homosexual spaces through the

molly house culture had a greater effect on the broader social constructions of gender and perceptions of homosexuality than any of its possible forebears. The molly houses created, in symbiosis with the broader London community and a changing heterosexuality, a homosexual character and caricature, which has exerted a profound influence on western attitudes towards homosexuality, and on the self image of later homosexuals. The molly houses became synonymous with homosexuality, and gradually over the course of the eighteenth and nineteenth centuries contributed to the broader transition, both in perception and reality, from the sodomite to the effeminate homosexual.[54]

Sodomy and slavery – sex on the slave ships

Returning to slavery, it is important to understand the incidences of sodomy and, or male rape, within this historical context of sexualities and the creation of sexual identities. Similarly any discussion of plantation homosexualities must be located within the wider context of the slave experience and must include the experiences aboard the slave ships. Walvin has described the horrific conditions aboard the slave ships in the following way:

It was the extremely high death-rate among the White sailors, the appalling conditions under which they worked and the brutality which even they were subjected which proved so persuasive in the abolition campaign against the slave trade . . . Their conditions of work and the regime of naval discipline were appalling on both military and mercantile ships, and sailors were themselves kept in some sort of order by the most draconian of punishments . . . it was hardly surprising that some of the crew on slavers found relief for their tension and sexual appetites with the slaves. Slave women were kept separately from the men. Most slave cargoes had fewer women and they were kept, with the child slaves, usually unshackled, in the smaller space between decks. They were an easy target, demoralized, defenceless and exposed to the passing whims of the White sailors. Sterner captains tried to keep their crews away from the women, but the men – already at sea for months past – were not so easily deflected. The sexual licence of the slave ships was, again, a telling factor in swinging opinion behind abolition after 1787. 'On board some ships the common sailor was allowed to have intercourse with such of the Black women whose consent they could procure. The officers are permitted to indulge their passions among them at pleasure, and sometimes are guilty of such brutal excesses, as disgrace human nature.'[55]

He continues,

> The brutality of sexual relations on the slave ships was only another aspect of the violence endemic throughout the slave trade. Sexually predatory sailors could effectively have their own way with the hapless slave victims . . . the crudity of sexuality on the slave ships established a pattern which was to recur throughout the slave colonies: of an unbridled and aggressive White sexuality towards slave women.[56]

Perhaps one can reasonably add slave men to the list!

In Dorsey's seminal piece on 'Patriarchy, Rape Culture and Slave-Body Semiotic', where he discusses rape as a 'learned behaviour' he quotes from *Middle Passage* by Charles Johnson: 'Didn't I say this was worse than prison? For another minute we stood waiting, looking at the door . . . as it opened and a heartbreakingly handsome cabin boy . . . came scrambling out . . . eyes crossed by what he'd been through.'[57]

The aforementioned point should be seen within the wider context of sexual activity between the planters. Gragg, in his study of the colonization of Barbados comments on homosexual activities between the planters:

> It is possible that the shortage of women contributed to homosexual relationships among some of the planters, although there is only slight documentary evidence. Hugh Evans and Thomas South, partners on a plantation in Christ Church parish, apparently had such a relationship. When Evans died in 1657, a man named Owin Shorte filed a deposition in which he explained that he had recently asked Evans if 'hee had got him a wife'. According to Shorte, Evans answered, 'hee had got all he intended'. Shorte understood Evans to mean that South was 'ye only wife hee desired'. Evans left South his entire estate.[58]

This discussion needs to consider the question of sex between the male slaves. Ransford, in his description of 'Hell in the Caribbean' writes of the alleged 'pigsty morals' and 'unnatural' activities between the slaves themselves:

> Indeed apart from singing and dancing there were few diversions left to the Negroes except fornication and sodomy, and opportunities for fornication were not always easy to come by. Half a life-time after he had escaped from slavery in the West Indies, a negro remembered how difficult it was to 'catch' a woman there, and he said that the majority of the men had to turn to pederasty: 'This was their life', he wrote, 'sodomy. The effeminate men washed the clothes and did the cooking too if they had a husband.' Nor did the Whites appreciate that a good deal of the promiscuity with women and the homosexualism, which they criticized so often, and with such disgust in their accounts of West Indian slavery, could in fact too be blamed to some extent on the planters' own prohibition of the taboos which in Africa had ordered the community life and kept it in many ways virtuous.[59]

In terms of sex between the male slaves and the planters, current research has not unearthed any accounts of forced rape or consensual sodomy between White slave masters and Black slaves. Dorsey's research into rape culture during slavery makes the valid admission that the only cases 'worthy' of archival documentation in nineteenth-century Cuba, for example, were cases involving free men of any colour. His discovery of three cases of consensual sodomy, between men in 1869, as against 42 of 'heterosexual rape' probably relates to free people. However, the detailed journals of Thomas Thistlewood on the Jamaican plantations, do contain physically abusive practices that can be located within a sado-masochistic or submission/domination matrix, common to some homosexual communities.

The Caribbean context and homosexualities

This deafening silence on homosexual abuse rings even more loudly within Burg's allegation of the near normativity of homosexuality in the Caribbean region. He writes:

Two hundred years before, in the early seventeenth century, homosexual acts were rarely condemned by anyone. They were ignored by ordinary citizens, officers of the church, the military, and by leaders of the civil government. Later on in the century, after the Civil War and the Interregnum, when Charles II was restored to the throne in 1660, homosexual acts and the men who committed them continued to attract little attention. Men who engaged other men for sexual purposes were found on every level of society, from the royal court, through the nobility, in the commercial classes, and on down to the sailors who manned the king's ships and the crews of the merchant fleet. For the most part, Englishmen regarded homosexual behaviour as simply another sexual activity, a peculiarity to some, a matter of jest to others, a thing for public cognizance when circumstances warranted, but mostly a practice to be ignored. Even for clerics and moralists profoundly concerned with sexual transgressions, homosexual activities were minor matters, no more dangerous than the heterosexual promiscuity they perceived to be corrupting the English nation. Amid the climate of toleration flourished one of the most unusual homosexually oriented groups in history, the Caribbean pirates who spread terror from South America northward to Bermuda and occasionally into the Pacific throughout the latter half of the seventeenth century.[60]

Burg posits the viewpoint that the pirate 'sodomic' tradition was different in that

> Among pirates, either aboard their ships or whilst living on isolated West Indian islands, homosexual acts were not integrated with or subordinated to alternate styles of sexual contact. They were the only form of sexual expression engaged in by members of the buccaneer community.[61]

He even suggests that the notorious Captain Morgan of Port Royal, Jamaica, did not abuse captured women – he 'neither raped nor brutalized' owing to his crew's homosexuality.[62]

The colonial milieu and homosexualities need to be seen in the global context of emerging colonial domination. Aldrich provokes further thought (or outrage) in his suggestion that it was not just Christianity, civilization and commerce that were factors in the 'colonial equation' but the 'gendered nature of overseas expansion, the ways in which sexual identities were constructed, evolving patterns of masculinity and the representation of sexuality in literature and art'.[63] In fact, according to Dorsey the only citations of homosexuality between White master and Black slave appear to be in 'historical novels of creative fiction' and not in 'historical documentation' such as 'archival sources'. In Aldrich's view, '(t)he colonies provided many possibilities for homoeroticism, homosociality and homosexuality – a variety of perspectives and experiences by which men expressed attraction to other men'.[64] In the preface of his book, he levels the accusation that

> [C]olonial lands which in the late nineteenth and early twentieth century included most of African, South and Southeast Asia, and the islands of the Pacific and Indian Oceans and the Caribbean, provide a haven for Europeans whose sexual inclinations did not fit neatly into the constraints of European society. Certain colonies became known as sites of homosexual license.[65]

Conclusion

It can be argued, though not wholly proven, that homosexual rape, as sodomy, was used as a weapon of subjugation of male slaves on the plantations. The resounding silence on such matters contrasts sharply with the historical accounts of heterosexual abuses inflicted on Black slave women and attests, not to its absence, but to its 'submerged' nature. Nevertheless, any discussion of homophobia among people of African-Caribbean descent must involve a thorough analysis of the history, social construct and culture of sodomy and homosexualities, which hopefully may uncover the truth.

In this brief exploration of the history of sexual behaviour as it relates to slavery, I have argued that it forms the backcloth for viewing homophobia within the history of sexualities and the possibility of there being historical underpinnings to contemporary homophobia in the African-Caribbean community. These observations are preliminary and further work needs to be undertaken. Moreover, further analysis will include a review of biblical interpretations as they contribute to homophobia or enable an understanding of Scripture that affirms people of various genders and sexual identities.

Other areas of study are signposted by the following

authors: Dyson, in his preface to his piece on homotextualities writes:

> The issue of homosexuality has reaped a whirlwind of controversy and acrimonious debate in most Christian communities. I believe that one of the explanations for Black homophobia is the realization that if heterosexuality – the supposed 'normal' sexuality – has been demonized in the West for centuries, then surely Black homosexuality will only up the ante of Black oppression. Thus, ironically enough, Blacks identify with mainstream sexual values – the very mainstream that has censored and castigated Black heterosexuality – when they practice homophobia. I am not arguing that homophobia has no homegrown Black varieties; I am simply suggesting that such homophobia allows Blacks to forge solidarity with a culture that has excluded them.[66]

Is homophobia a desire for 'respect' and inclusion within White heterosexual elites? The substantive point of this question is amplified by Horace Griffin who states

> African Americans are typically unaware that a large part of their sexual understanding and sense of sexual morality is a result of their English Christian social order imposed on them in this country during the last three centuries. Bill Piersen, a historian of African American culture, documents the fact that [Africans] found many of their standards of morality and pre-marital sexual mores rejected out of hand by the puritanical master class . . . many of the Afro-American sexual relationships that appalled Christian observers as immoral deviations of monogamy were in reality attempts to blend African mores with the new social realities of American bondage.[67]

This leads to a further question: Are our ancestors' sexualities more relevant to our lives in the twenty-first century than nineteenth-century Greco-Roman biblical ethics, interpreted by Western racists? Writing on sexuality and spirituality, Kelly Brown Douglas, quoting Peter Paris, notes that 'secularity has no reality in the African experience . . . This is why many African cultures did not view sexual intercourse as bad or evil, but celebrated this part of life . . . in the final analysis, human sexuality makes human relationships possible – including the relationship to the divine.'[68]

The question that arises from this quotation is: Have we fallen victim to the West's concept of 'religion' that separates body from spirit?

Kwok Pui-Lan raises the pertinent issue of how 'theology has *colonized* the field of religious studies, which is simply another concrete example of Christian imperialism. Consequently, Christianity continues to serve as the prototype of a religion, and the standard for evaluating other wisdom traditions.'[69] So a significant question in this discourse remains: Has Christianity demonized a form of sexual expression within the diaspora that falls within the sacredness of African traditions?

9. Spinning Theology: Trickster, Texts and Theology

MICHAEL N. JAGESSAR

> I have plucked my Anancy from the great folk tales of West Africa
> and the Caribbean and I have made him inhabit both worlds,
> the old and the new locked deep down in my imagination . . .
> Andrew Salkey, *Anancy Score* (1973), p. 7

> Master of the crossroads, the Anancy artist provokes that dialogue
> which brings creative disorder into the oppressive structures
> that dehumanise our world.
> Joyce Jonas, *Anancy in the Great House* (1990), pp. 12–13

Theology with a view: tapping epics from the cosmic floor

In this chapter I will explore the metaphor of 'trickster' in
relation to texts and Caribbean (and Black) God-talk and
its implications for 'colouring' or 'spinning' theology. This
piece is part of my larger agenda of reclaiming Anancy as a
conversation partner in doing theology.

I like the notion of 'theologizing with a view' as this act
involves a 'bringing into view' our multiple take or spin on
God, God's purposes and God's grace working in human
existence.[1] For theology is the encounter of *theos* (God) –
through the word revealed in Scripture and especially in the
Word made flesh in Christ – and *logos*, the words of a people
and the harsh realities of their lived experiences.[2] Theology,
or more precisely God-talk, is always a work of faith insepar-
able from the lived experiences of the everyday life, and it
ought to point towards liberative transformation.

Such *em-body-ing* of theology can never claim to be noetic or objective, especially if objectivity means 'keeping a safe emotional and cognitive distance from the subject matter' and/or a 'neutral stance'.[3] Whatever the tools, techniques and scholarship one employs in theologizing, and whatever the role of the Spirit, our articulation will reflect the culture, social location, gender, ethnicity and theology (*inter alia*) that have shaped and continue to shape us.[4] This is besides the fact that the biblical texts are culturally and ideologically conditioned.[5] In the framework of contextual biblical hermeneutics, Elsa Tamez succinctly puts the issue this way:

> [W]e begin with our context and the context orients the exegete or the common reader to choose those texts that are a lamp to the feet and a light for the path. Manipulation? Antiscientific? No. It is the desperate need to grasp onto a light for a particular situation.[6]

I have yet to meet a disembodied theologian or hermeneut. We all read, listen and theologize with a view, however much we strive to remain faithful to technique, content and theology. This is especially the case with Black[7] people, for whom God is not a theological dictum. God, who is intimately involved in their lives as a marginalized people, is in the thick and thin of every corner of their existence in very specific ways.[8]

As one whose life has been shaped in the Caribbean, my theology, theologizing and hermeneutics reflects its Caribbean heritage – especially its rainbow nature. This is one of the reasons why I find it difficult to theologize with *a* view. Like Anancy, my proclivity is to do theology from a multiplicity of views, that is, 'with eight legs tapping epics from the cosmic floor'.[9]

Spinning webs of bright imagining: Anancy, the signifying spider

In my theological pilgrimage I have been led to rediscover Anancy, the patron saint of Caribbean peoples, as a conversation partner in the task of digging deep into texts (written and oral), lives and the existential contexts of peoples of the Caribbean, within and beyond the geographical demarcation of the region. In Anancy I find a dialogue partner and an ideal, albeit ambivalent, voice to employ in doing theology in/through the form of narrative or story. In attempting to reread the biblical texts and theological notions alongside Caribbean and Caribbean diaspora[10] textual sources and lives, I want to lift Anancy from Caribbean/African folklore and employ him/her as the medium to converse and engage with these texts and notions from a multiplicity of optics simultaneously.

My motivation for this comes from three interrelated impulses. The first is from the example of Andrew Salkey and his work in the volume *Anancy Score* (1973). Salkey's attempt to locate Anancy as a 'dweller' in, between and bridging two or three worlds is still relevant to Caribbean communities in general and theological discourse in such contexts in particular. Caribbean peoples have lived, and are living, in and around what Gloria Anzaldúa refers to as 'the borderlands'.[11] It seems to me that this is an apt paradigm for God-talk or any articulation of the mystery of the divine.

My second motivation is derived from the challenge posed by another Caribbean writer, Wilson Harris. That is, to create new forms and characters based on the dialogue of cultures (including cultural hybridity) rather than becoming locked into texts, methods and characters that perpetuate static configurations of culture, identity, ethnicity, colour and gender. This, according to Harris, calls for a 'literacy of the imagination' as a means to uncover what is eclipsed by the dominant culture.[12] In my view this is as much a project for Caribbean literature as it is a challenge for theological discourse in the Caribbean and the Caribbean diaspora around the North Atlantic world.

The latter leads me to my third motivation which is the desire to find a culture-specific (that is Caribbean) trope that would engender vistas for unrestricted theological discourse in the context of ethnic and religious diversity. Anancy opens up the possibility of drawing from a pool of 'cultural' signifiers that one can plunge into and bring out 'a unique crystallization, a new text with a unique texture and fresh context'.[13] Moreover, I am excited by the ripe possibilities implied in the paradigm of Anancy, the signifying spider spinning webs – of identities, cultures, languages, religions – with 'its numerous circuits and multiple interconnections'.[14]

My overall concern is to locate a voice and form that speaks to my historical and cultural contexts – both as a person from the Caribbean and a member of the Caribbean diaspora. Anancy and 'Anancyism' is for me a timely paradigm that opens new vistas into the dynamic nature of 'cultural creolization'[15] – the kind of necessary accommodation and synthesis that occurs as minority communities, through negotiation, create necessary symbolic spaces to allow their religious rituals and other cultural expressions to adapt creatively to new environments.[16] This is a crucial insight for theological discourse among members of the Caribbean diasporas and I note particularly its relevance for Black theology in Britain.

Anancy is an appropriate cultural and discursive partner in deconstructing the myth of objective, verifiable and logical truth that so much of Christianity is locked into. Here the insight of J. C. Conroy and R. A. Davis on education in Britain can help elucidate my point. They argue a case for the 'trickster figure' in the classroom to counter 'the development of an over-dependence upon an *arithmetic calculus* as the primary mythic' in the British culture.[17] My point is that Anancy (the trickster) can serve as a liberating paradigm to counter such overdependence and to enable listeners in marginal communities to release some of the biblical texts and theological notions from the shackles of ideological and cultural captivity in order to become relevant in the present context. Moreover, as Anancy discourse is 'a trans-national catch of signifiers and signifieds – spinning – always producing new formations',[18] 'Anancyism' can become a symbol for Caribbean cultural continuity and identities that are continuously reworked in the diaspora. Recognizing the cultural specificity of the Anancy optics, it is still my hope that readers from across different cultures may be able to identify with Anancy and her discourse.

Locating Anancy

Who or what is Anancy? Anancy (also referred to as Anansi, Ananse or Nanzi)[19] stories are told throughout the Caribbean and among the Caribbean diaspora.[20] These stories can be referred to as the Caribbean version of oral wisdom sayings/writings. Anancy, the descendant of a West African deity, takes on special significance in the context of Caribbean history. As Joyce Jonas notes, 'the spider of Ashanti folklore, survived the middle passage, and still spins his yarns throughout the Caribbean' (and beyond) – hiding 'in rafters' and 'any nook or cranny'.[21] According to Jonas, this has been possible because of Anancy's

> capacity to transform disruption, discontinuity, brokenness, and defeat into triumphant new configurations of possibility. His perennial rebellion and his use of comic trickery and deceit to expose the inadequacies of authority figures must surely have endeared him to the imagination of a downtrodden people.[22]

Anancy is hero and villain, loveable and trickster, wily and stupid, wisdom's genius, subtle and uncouth, God's mouthpiece and rival, and is known to live by wits. Anancy is often portrayed as shrewd, laid-back and with many of his/her[23] tricks aimed at all aspects of life. Humour is a key characteristic as the tricks are directed towards turning upside down the systemic oppression and oppressive situations or to hint at situations where such oppression is not overtly evident. Anancy is no respecter of the sacred and challenges the gods 'not so much in defiance as in a new ordering of their limits'.[24] Diane J. Austin-Broos, for instance, notes that by employing 'the enigma of play', Anancy challenges God's role (rather than God) 'as the moral nexus for the world of work' by unearthing 'sensuousness and fallibility of a rational world' to puncture the 'logic of moral discipline applied to the notion of labouring self'.[25] But whether in defiance of the sacred or tricking humans, Anancy, 'an agent of ambiguity', brings contradiction into human life, serving as both 'a medium of coherence and incoherence'.[26] In the process Anancy engenders a 'dialectic whose aim is not synthesis but a never-ending juggling of thesis and anti-thesis'.[27] She opens up *spaces* where play, difference, transformation and paradox can live together.

Anancy is the great survivor who wears innumerable masks that represent the behaviour and state of affairs of human beings. Anancy's negotiating of multiple identities and her in-between-ness underscores the multi-layered dimensions of human life. Whatever the mask, Anancy embodies the manifoldness of what *is*. Anancy takes different shapes: human form, insect and animal forms. As web-spinner taking refuge in the ceiling,[28] Anancy 'weaves a Calibanesque web and spins a signifyin(g) discourse',[29] deconstructing and reconstructing language, texts and stories. Anancy is varied, ambivalent, sometimes a figure of hope, a model of how to survive and a voice of subversion. Wanderer at the crossroads, inhabitant of limbo spaces, Anancy is never locked in a prescribed location or enclosure and yet is never outside it.[30] This ambivalence is further attested by the fact that Anancy can be the person named 'peacefulness', as well as the trickster in the form of a politician, business person or preacher![31] The point is: whatever the physical embodiment (or mask), Anancy flouts categorization 'in order to retain his[/her] indeterminacy'.[32] Anancy, the trickster, as Robert Pelton writes,

> enters the human world to make things happen, to recreate boundaries, to break and re-establish relationships, to reawaken consciousness of the presence and the creative power of both the sacred Center and the formless outside. Then he [she] returns to that hidden threshold which he [she] embodies and makes available as a passage 'to save people from ruin'.[33]

Like other cultural 'icons' that are part of diasporic peoples' history, Anancy or Anancyism has become more than an Ashanti folklore. It symbolizes 'the creative result of a trans-national phenomenon passing through densely layered local circumstances',[34] or what was earlier referred to as the nature of cultural creolization.

The trickster in storytelling or narrative[35]

It is evident that the Anancy folk stories fall into the genre of 'trickster' tales or narratives. The trickster figure or character appears in folktales and myths of many cultures and peoples[36] usually, though not always, located in the 'animal tales' genre. Of significance is the shared feature of a small size in comparison to the bigger and stronger animals that appear in the same stories. At the heart of the folklores of oppressed people is 'the ability of the weak to survive through cunning, trickery and sheer deception in an environment of the strong and powerful'.[37] Trickster tales/narratives, through mockery, trickery and mystery, enable oppressed human beings to subvert dominance and subjugation and survive the overwhelming and uncontrollable agents of death in their lives. These tales[38] are closely linked to the rhetorical practice known as 'signifying' and generally serve satirical or parodic purposes by poking fun at various human behaviours.[39]

Trickster figures are wise and their ability to laugh at the troubles they stir is related to the desire to challenge the appearance of existential realities and transform/transcend situations of hopelessness and contradictions. They can level the playing field in an instant and bring laughter or playfulness to an oppressed people in an oppressive situation. They are the very 'embodiment of paradox'[40] with the ability to move 'between symbolic categories of being and action, changing shape and identity in order to expose and redress various deep-seated human follies'.[41]

In *The Trickster in West Africa* (1980) Pelton suggests that the trickster should be perceived as a symbolic pattern embodying the transforming power of the human imagination – playing with relationships and creating images of the world. Embodied in the trickster is the irregular and the structured, the sacrosanct and the irreverent, the incongruous and the significant coupled to create 'an image of irony and of the working of the ironic imagination itself'.[42] Incarnated into a diversity of cultures, the 'oxymoronic imagination' of the trickster playfully fools around beyond boundaries, structures and rules to discover 'new paradigms' and 'new logics'.[43] As an agent of acts of transgression, the trickster does more than merely violate the sacred codes/boundaries and engender chaos. She also 'initiates a transformative process' that facilitates 'contradictory elements into a web of meaningful relationships'.[44]

The word grew eight legs: biblical precedents

The question for my purpose, however, is this: Is there a connection with the trickster figure in the biblical narratives? The Bible, quintessentially a book of stories, is replete with underdog tales and the trickster as subtype of the underdog. The trickster/underdog type, as Susan Niditch observes, 'held special appeal for the Israelite composers who shaped the tales of their ancestral heroes; for throughout its history, Israel has had a peculiar self-image as the underdog and the trickster'.[45] Niditch goes on to define a trickster as a 'fascinating and universal folk hero' who 'brings about a change in a situation via trickery',[46] employing wit and cunning in the place of his/her marginal location and non-existent power base.

Drawing upon the idea of 'trickster stories as comedy inviting laughter to celebrate the trick', Melissa Jackson goes further than Niditch to argue that trickster narratives in the Bible 'belong to a comic genre' and that the history of hermeneutics 'has moved from viewing these passages comically'.[47] Her conclusion, however, that through the subversive comic lens readers can discern a reversed reality without tricksters as there are no underdogs, is contestable. This, in my view, diminishes the 'real' oppression in a patriarchal society and specifically the oppression of women, children and the foreigner/Other in the biblical narratives.

No doubt, humour and the comic are significant dimensions to trickster stories in the Hebrew Bible and in the stories of many other peoples. I agree, however, with Niditch that in the Bible the 'trickster morphology has an anti-establishment quality at the very source of its being'.[48] In oppressive and desperate situations the trickster interrupts to subvert the status quo, to contradict, to undermine expectations and to puncture/overthrow human hubris,[49] while in the process highlighting the absurdity and inconsistency of what may be perceived. In other words, 'things are definitely not as they seem'.[50]

From a biblical/theological perspective, it is in the context of the biblical storytellers' use of trickster as a subtype that I am proposing to transpose and translate Anancy into the Christian context of theology and hermeneutics. Taking my cue from Andrew Salkey, who has reworked the Anancy paradigm in Caribbean folk stories for a contemporary Caribbean[51] audience and from the biblical use of the trickster, I contend that Caribbeans at 'home' and beyond, especially in the Caribbean diaspora communities across the Atlantic, can reclaim and reinvent the Anancy paradigm in context(s) of totalizing proclivity, calculus dominance and logical obsession, to stir the theological imaginations of folks towards subversive and/or tactical readings of key texts, notions and stories.

I am aware of the problematic that trickster stories defeat attempts of appropriation as they call into question notions of identity and property that defy the very idea of owner-ship.[52] And, at the same time, the trickster figure has the ability to move across and between cultures and to provide more liberating metaphors than the fossilized ones we are locked into.[53] It is my view, that the ability to cross and trans-gress cultural and other boundaries may be located in diverse peoples having in common a complex, web-like nature of human relationships and cultural interaction rather than the futile obsession with the 'pure' and 'homogenous' (be it ethnicity, culture, religion, etc.).[54]

It is precisely because of this ability to transgress cultures and the inability to 'lock' the trickster into a monolithic mould that I find in Anancy an ideal conversation partner in the much-needed exercise of retelling/telling and resurfacing the narratives of marginalized and oppressed folks,[55] inhabit-ing the crossroads or borderlands of religions,[56] wrestling with issues of identities, cultures, religion and in the urgent task of finding, liberating and transforming new ways of speaking of and representing the divine.

Spinning theological threads – insights from Anancy, the story-weaver

The Anancy paradigm will allow me to draw freely on the breadth of the historical and socio-cultural context of Caribbean diversity as significant optics.[57] As a dialogue part-ner, Anancy will assist me, the 'hermeneut', to use Caribbean frame(s) of reference to bring alive and relevantly decon-struct, reconstruct and appropriate particular texts and theo-logical notions. This is a 'subjective' exercise and cannot claim to be otherwise. It is premised on the conviction that reading habits are contextual, with the recognition that the context is not a static and homogenous location. *Multiversity* is the operative word. Consequently, there is the inbuilt recognition that this reading is offering only a partial view on the biblical texts and theological notions under examination and in doing so relates to the particular context and experiences of Caribbean peoples. This is not to diminish any relevance and implications for other peoples with similar experiences of the possibilities for intercultural dialogues.

What, then, are some of the nascent insights from Anancy/Anancyism for theologizing or doing and thinking theology? In the specific context of the Caribbean and the Caribbean diaspora, can Anancy, as a dialogue partner and 'Anancyism' as a heuristic, engender a releasing of the theological imagination to imagine new and fruitful discourses? Can Anancy, dweller at crossroads and child of ambivalence, challenge and rouse our monolithic constructs of theological notions, jump-starting the maverick in these and point to new possibilities of articulating and crafting pertinent theological discourses for today?[58]

Let me interject here a key reasoning for repositioning Anancy in Caribbean diasporic and Black theological discourse. Having inherited Christianity with all its Western Eurocentric baggage, I suggest that we have become locked into a largely Protestant theological mindset that has relegated the act of the imagination to the realm of 'hocus-pocus' which is viewed with much suspicion. While Black theological discourses (and contextual theologies) emphasize experience, there is still much work to be done in the area of 'imagination'.

Consequently, a trickster figure, such as Anancy, is seen as the devil incarnate and would never be associated with anything religious, particularly Christian – at least not on Sunday mornings and at theological schools! In effect, Caribbean Christians have bought into the Eurocentric enterprise of relegating the ambiguities and contradictions of life into some 'lockdown' corner in order to settle the questions quickly 'with answers that accentuate certitude and truth'.[59] In fact, Black theological discourse in the UK, the Caribbean and throughout the Caribbean diaspora is yet to engage with the notion of 'truth' in Christianity and in other religions. Further, Black (especially Pentecostal) theological discourse is still locked into a narrow reading of the biblical texts.

I will now highlight five 'threads of insight' that constitute my case for employing the 'Anancy' paradigm as a dialogue partner in theological discourse.

Alter-*native* talk and multiplicity of voices

I am working with a notion of theology as God-talk or language about God. God-talk is risky engagement given the mysterious nature of God. For who dares to speak of God with certainty? Yet many have done and continue to do so. Moreover, the language we employ is always a human construct.[60] What the foregoing implies is the tentative nature of such discourses and the demand for humility upon the individual and the community as theologizing is not an individual labour. Whatever the 'spin' reflected in our God-talk, which is fed by our multifarious lived experiences in the first instance, the fact remains that 'for now we see in a mirror dimly' (1 Cor. 13.12). This is not to diminish the fact that there has been and is oppressive God-talk and blatantly 'bad theology' that must be critiqued. There are numerous examples where in our theologizing/God-talk, like the friends of Job, we 'have not spoken of [God] what is right' (Job 62.7)

It is for this reason that I subscribe to the view that theologizing or God-talk is necessarily a counter-discourse to the dominant discourse of the world/establishment. It is the daringness to speak in voicing and sustaining an alter-*native* talk.[61] A commitment to this agency is giving theological content to what Kamau Brathwaithe refers to as 'nation language'.[62] Anancy/Anancyism offers me one way to plumb this counter-discourse in the context of the Caribbean and the Caribbean diaspora communities. Anancy is able to play a multiplicity of voices, creating the necessary *space* to enable the voices and languages, eclipsed by the dominant, to be unearthed or surfaced. Here it is timely to note that my emphasis is on '*space*' as against '*place*'.[63] Entering the 'architectonic' fossil spaces of time[64] like archaeologists, Anancy theologizing subverts, mocks and tricks.[65] In the process the voices are liberated to imagine an alter-*native* or counter-discourse geared towards mediating the overthrowing of the powers. Theologizing or God-talk, like Caribbean stories, becomes an 'emblematic detour' reflected in a method of counter-values or *sub-version*.[66]

Resistance rhetoric and a counter-imagination

Resistance[67] rhetorics hold a central place in Caribbean and Black peoples experiences of oppression. This is evident in their oral tradition of storytelling and folklore, cultural forms such as carnivals and folk dances, their music (and lyrics), popular religiosity, and their use of language in the literary forms of poetry and narrative. Hence, this is more than speech; the performative is an integral part of the resistance. And resistance, according to Vincent Wimbush,

> is necessarily a response to, and in its varied expressions partly determined by, the varied manifestations of power. The realm of the imaginary, the visionary, the utopic is discovered and cultivated by those who define themselves as pressed and limited in some significant ways by power, as a means of resisting such power.[68]

In his analysis of the dynamics of power and resistance between dominant and dominated groups, James C. Scott highlights how the subjugated or subaltern 'adopt[s] a strategic pose in the presence of the powerful'.[69] Anger, umbrage, dislike and rage are masked by various acts of accommodation that trick the dominant group into believing that their hegemony is accepted. This is the 'public transcript'. The need to talk back, however, is always simmering behind or underneath those masks and, as a consequence of this need, the dominated creates a 'hidden transcript' that camouflages their critique of the dominant power. These 'arts of resistance' take various forms: jokes, speech, songs, carnival, linguistic tricks, gossips, euphemisms, grumbling, folktales, the rhetorical and the imaginary, among others.[70]

Anancy's world is within the 'arts or tactics of resistance'. It is through these that she will spin theological discourses to subvert the 'lie' of dominant theological discourses. The Anancy paradigm offers a ripe *space* for nurturing a counter-imagination in a context of what Wilson Harris calls 'the illiteracy of the imagination'. Imagining differently anchors Caribbean and Black folks' struggle to be self-defining – to own their heritage and experiences as they dream a present and a future that is grounded on hope. Anancy makes dramatic use of *memory* or *the act of recalling* towards creating a new possibility or reality. She/he can provide memories, narratives, visions, images and metaphors that are not easily domesticated. These can enable us to imagine worlds where ideas and stories are restaged/rehearsed and dialogue and cross-fertilize across cultural boundaries. Hence, it is possible for the Anancy paradigm to offer more useful, dynamic and cathartic metaphors than those we are accustomed to. These linger in the hearing and the talking and offer possibilities for imagining a 'new heaven and a new earth' – the 'more' of a world transformed.

There is, of course, a biblical precedence for this. The process of imagining or tapping into the imagination of God is akin to the *midrash*[71] hermeneutic process. Here the biblical text is pushed beyond limits and outside the boundaries, extended or elaborated, turned upside down and inside out as 'truth' gets broken and rearranged. What is not said in the text becomes just as significant as what is said. In the process, meanings and insights never imagined and perceived before become evident. Like the *midrash*, the Anancy paradigm enables us to liberate and release the imagination and give

God and the Spirit more latitude or space to move freely within the texts (especially at the edges or boundaries),[72] the context of the text, the reading community and the context of the reading community.

Spinning between lines: tricking words, playful language

Language, in the case of peoples of the Caribbean and the Caribbean diaspora, has been and still is someone else's language, that is, the language of the dominant group. Hence, our worship of God and our engagement in theological discourse is still alien to our souls.[73] A. Sivanandan puts the dilemma this way: '[H]ow does one express the holiness of the heart's disaffection and "the truth of the imagination" in a language that is false to one? How does one communicate the burden of one's humanity in a language that dehumanises one in the very act of communication?'[74] This is the very dilemma that Walcott highlights: the tension between his love for both his African and English tongue. Should he 'betray them both or give them back what they give'?[75]

A counter-imagination demands of the 'dominated' a skilful corruption or tricking of grammar, syntax and vocabulary in order to 'blacken the language, suffuse it with [one's] own darkness and liberate it from the presence of the oppressor'.[76] Hence, the inversion and 'splitting up' of words, their ordering and grammar through sounds, musicality, rhythm and 'playing' with words.

Language, as used by Anancy, is located in this project to skilfully subvert the status quo. As noted earlier, it is in the use of language that trickster stories open a way in the more profound wisdom of who we are, about our world(s) and about the divine. Through 'punning, ever troping, ever embodying the ambiguities of language'[77] and subverting language and its semiotic elements, Anancy beckons us to perceive the world differently: to hear, retell, contradict, reweave and to imagine new and alter-*native* stories. The insignificant '*Anancy seh* (says)' in my Anancy theological discourses, points to this liberating potential.

Within the wider scope of my theological 'spin' is the conviction that God-talk or theologizing finds an authentic home in the figurative, metaphorical and mythic. Here one can learn from the other religious traditions, especially Hinduism and Buddhism, which remind us with acuity that in our God-talk we would do well to remember that words are 'fingers that point to the moon'.[78] The power of words lies in what they are pointing to rather than in the words. Troy Wilson Organ expresses the idea very well: 'Theology is best understood as an art form. It uses myths, parables, and oxymorons. Theology deceives when interpreted literally, but it deceives truly when it is interpreted symbolically. Religious language fails when it succeeds, and succeeds when it fails.'[79]

Strictly speaking, Anancy shifts the focus from inordinate emphasis on the written text to the community in conversation. Her/his style depends on the force of words, sounds, songs, speeches, rhythm and the displacement of traditional grammatical structures for its impact on the listeners.[80] This is why a volume in print can be seen as contradiction. DeSouza correctly notes that the signifyin(g) potential of the trickster story is not only lost to listeners who are not part of the community, but *also* by relying on the written form of transmission.[81] Mindful of this caveat, it is my hope (in the tradition of Salkey, Agard and others) that in the act of reading, readers would become fully engaged – drawn into the retelling, reweaving and reimagining. The texts that readers look at become texts that they look through. In other words, the texts become 'performative', active and alive, working like yeast on readers to consider, to interrogate,[82] and to create alternative spaces for new eyes for seeing, new ears for hearing and new hearts for listening and joining in the discourse. It is similar to what Hans Reudi-Weber refers to when he wrote of the Bible as 'the book that reads me'.[83]

In the complex worlds of many of the descendents of the Caribbean diaspora, I suggest that the Anancy paradigm is quite suited to release the full and fresh potential of words, to craft new words and semantics, and to imagine words (and worlds) connected to the drama of Black lives. Words and speech enable the community to rediscover the power, depth and intensity of the heart.

Anancy's language invites listeners to hear a multiplicity of voices as the stories, alongside past and present stories and history, are remembered, retold and reimagined. Meaning is characterized by fluidity and is open to negotiation. In this context, Anancy's speech/language must be truly a counter-discourse to ensure that it does not in itself become another form of oppression. Moreover, for descendants of the Caribbean diaspora language takes on an added dimension, as they wrestle with the attempt 'to create identities that defy the border of the modern construct of the western nation/state'.[84] In a continual state of wandering from one nation to another and where home is elsewhere, language becomes a significant homeland.[85] Anancy, the wordsmith, border-crosser, expert at negotiating gateways and the state of in-between-ness, has much to offer in this regard, especially in creating alter-*native* spaces of subversive autonomy and freedom for Black folks and the concomitant implications for theologizing.

Anancy and the mimetic

Many years ago, Harvey Cox made a significant contribution to theological discourse (which was way ahead of its time) when he wrote *The Feast of Fools* (1969). Lamenting the quarantining of parody, the loss of the comic sensibility, and the separation of politics from imagination,[86] Cox provided a timely theological treatise on festivity and fantasy contending that the human is both *homo festivus* and *homo fantasia*.[87] He goes on to underscore the trickster aspects in Jesus who is in constant dissonance with the status quo:

Like the jester, Christ defies custom and scorns crowned heads. Like a wandering troubadour he has no place to lay his head. Like the clown in the circus parade, he satirizes existing authority by riding into town replete with regal pageantry when he has no earthly power. Like a minstrel he frequents dinners and parties. At the end he is costumed by his enemies in a mocking caricature of royal paraphernalia. He is crucified . . . with a sign over his head that lampoons his laughable claim.[88]

As trickster or harlequin, as Cox posits, Christ embodies 'the spirit of play in a world of calculated utilitarian seriousness'[89] that juxtaposes the comic and the serious and 'is enriched by his mimicry'.[90]

Mimicry is more than mere imitation. Gerard Aching rightly argues that this complex practice in the Caribbean be viewed 'as a means of shifting power relations', that employs 'partially hidden public spaces' to practise politics of freedom 'on a lower frequency'.[91] Recently, Marion Grau, in proposing 'a Christology of divine commerce',[92] highlights the significance of 'a trickster-like Christ [who] mimics and mocks the boundaries of ownership and slavery'.[93] Thus,

This scandalously different Christ, a rather suspect and marginal 'persona' or mask for divine agency, appears, then, as holy fool, divine trickster. Deceiving the devil, counterfeiting the counterfeiters, Christ the Counterfeiter might help us invent ways to unveil and resist the con men of our time.[94]

Grau draws heavily on Homi Bhabha's theorizing on ambivalence and mimicry in colonial discourse[95] to argue her case for a 'model of *imitatio christi*' that will enthuse 'redemptive strategies of faithful tricksterdom and holy foolery'.[96] Hence, in her contrapuntal reading of Jesus' kingdom parables alongside the notion of the mimetic, she is able to identify mimicry at work in these as the parables 'obliquely represent' what is then the current economic context, 'while mocking embedded assumptions about power, hierarchy, and gender'.[97] As Bhabha contends, the mimetic, 'signs of spectacular resistance', represents *'almost the same, but not quite the same'*.[98]

Long before Bhabha's and Grau's theorizing on the notion of the mimetic, however, the use of mimicry in Caribbean experiences and among peoples of the Caribbean diaspora has been in operation, especially in the areas of literature and popular religion. Theorists of such a notion (and other notions, such as ambivalence, language, culture and identity) can profit by becoming familiar with the Caribbean input. It is precisely here that my insertion of the Anancy trajectory can contribute to this necessary conversation, albeit in the context of an interdisciplinary approach to theologizing.

Anancy, as a performer of mimicry and ambivalence 'performs perfidy', 'provides a hermeneutic of hyperbole, a syntax of sarcasm; and invents idioms of irony'[99] to threaten, transgress, trick and subvert the lie of our neat and fossilized dogmas, our obsession with the need for quick answers to complex questions driven by our illusionary charade of certainty. In questioning our representation of the sacred and the divine, Anancy and her mimicry offers a way into the world of ambivalence, walking the tightrope of chaos and living with the 'messy economies of our world',[100] precisely where authentic God-talk is birthed, lives and breathes.

Once upon an umbilical time: the story-weaver

This project of 'releasing' Anancy into the world of theological discourse also has a heuristic function in the ongoing exercise of affirming the centrality of stories, narratives and storytelling in doing theology. Theology is already dead when divorced from people's history, existential realities and real-life stories. Sallie McFague underscores this point: 'Where theology becomes overtly abstract, conceptual and systematic, it separates thought and life, belief and practice, words and their embodiment, making it more difficult, if not impossible, for us to believe in our hearts what we confess with our lips.'[101] Vital theology plumbs the depths of a people's life and living – witnessing to God's anguish in people's anguish, celebrating God's hope in the hopes of a people, pointing to God's anger in people's anger and connecting God's laughter with people's laughter.[102]

Caribbean peoples are a storytelling, story-listening and story-making people. Stories and storytelling are especially significant for people with a heritage of multiple displacements such as the Caribbean. As mentioned before, for people for whom home has always been 'elsewhere' story and language become powerful means of homecoming.[103] Narratives or stories are a powerful and essential means of communicating life experiences and the place of God-talk in these experiences. They communicate depth and complexity and offer space for ambiguity and multiversity in interpretation and imaging. Be it in the Caribbean or in the Caribbean diaspora around the North Atlantic world, Caribbeans can reel out stories of the demonic, of triumphs and defeats, and of promises realized, hopes smashed and dreams held on to. Reflected in these is the power and grace that transcends human ambiguities. What can be more theological than these? It is a not a choice we make when it comes to theologizing. It is the way God-talk or discourse comes to us in the earthy/messy stories of our existential encounters.

Anancy, the story-weaver, can help us reclaim the central place of storytelling in doing theology in the Caribbean and in the context of the Caribbean diaspora. It also has the possibility of becoming a powerful transforming tool with the ability to oppose and subvert prejudices built in Caribbean stories. In engaging the mind and the heart, Anancy points to why something is or is not (so) in a circumventing way. This can be done in a way that re-engages, rereads and revisions the biblical stories and discourse on theological ideas/themes in the specific context(s) of the experiences of peoples of the Caribbean and the Caribbean diaspora. Through this trajectory, biblical stories and theological notions are released from the printed texts and pages/documents, and in the process characters, as well as beginnings, endings and futures are invented and re-imagined. Stories, moreover, work their own miracles; one cannot lay claims on them as one's exclusive property even though they evolve from one's own experiences. The fact that they are told and shared is an open invitation for others to weave their own stories into the interconnectedness of the human condition. The real challenge is whether we are adventurous enough to trust that the divine will preserve the integrity of it all.

Limb-bow dancing and rain-bow theologizing

Like a trickster-thief, Anancy borrows from a diverse Caribbean heritage and beyond, blurs and crosses boundaries, and tentatively appropriates to release biblical texts and theological notions from bondage. Like a shaman, Anancy stirs in us a sense of mystery, a desire to make the texts, notions and stories 'strange again', and to think of what is not. Like a seamstress, Anancy stitches or weaves together the unusual of the ordinary to release us from our narrowly locked perceptions of life, identities, and the Lover-God in our midst to point towards richer ways of apprehending the divine and her purposes for all of creation. Like a liberating boundary-crosser, Anancy releases our 'versions of truth' from the perfect moulds and the sanitized chambers we have locked these into, freeing us from our rigidly neat propositions to discovering 'truth' in the juicy, earthy and sticky stories of our relational encounters with people, creation and the Delighter-God.[104]

To paraphrase John Agard: With head perched in the mountains of Jamaica and the Guyanas, knees spread wide in Africa, neck arched somewhere in Haiti and Brazil, toes touching Uttar Pradesh and Liberia, hands cleaving the air and sands in Iraq, legs shaped bowlike across the UK and

Europe, and the whole body dancing to and fro multiple worlds in excitement,[105] Anancy theologizing, hermeneutics and storytelling are capable of bending backwards over and forward under, of experiencing multiple somersaults in multiple directions, of imaging and sustaining an imagination of hope-full theologizing; an act that is full of ripe possibilities and curves like an expectant mother ready to give birth.

This is limbo-dancing theologizing, and it is my hope that the stories or discourses that evolve from this method will catch moments that may open up creative spaces to break through our rigidity and unnecessary theological polarizations. Anancy discourses do not pretend to give quick answers to our complex lives and contexts. They will merely highlight the sharp, contradictory and complex nature of faith and faithfulness and the need for a multiversity approach to theologizing.

Notes

Introduction

1 Robert Beckford, *Jesus Is Dread: Black Theology and Black Culture in Britain*, London: Darton, Longman & Todd, 1998.

2 Paul Grant and Raj Patel (eds), *A Time to Speak: Perspectives of Black Christians in Britain*, Birmingham: A Joint Publication of 'Racial Justice' and the 'Black Theology Working Group', 1990.

3 Paul Grant and Raj Patel (eds), *A Time to Act: Kairos 1992*, Birmingham: A Joint Publication of 'Racial Justice' and the 'Black and Third World Theology Working Group', 1992.

4 See chapter 5 of Anthony G. Reddie, *Black Theology in Transatlantic Dialogue*, New York: Palgrave, 2006.

5 A. A. Sivanandan, *A Different Hunger: Writings on Black Resistance*, London: Pluto Press, 1982.

6 Ron Ramdin, *The Making of the Black Working Class*, London: Gower, 1987.

7 Kobener Mercer, *Welcome to the Jungle*, London and New York: Routledge, 1994.

8 Among R. S. Sugirtharajah's many publications see *Postcolonial Criticism and Biblical Interpretation*, London: Oxford University Press, 2002.

9 Among Stuart Hall's many publications see *The Hard Road to Renewal: Thatcherism and the Crisis of the Left*, London: Verso, 1988.

10 John Wilkinson, James H. Evans Jr and Renate Wilkinson, *Inheritors Together*, London: Race, Pluralism and Community Group of the Board for Social Responsibility of the Church of England, 1985, p. 10.

11 Henry H. Mitchell, *Black Church Beginnings: The Long-Hidden Realities of the First Years*, Grand Rapids, Michigan/ Cambridge, UK: W. B. Eerdmans, 2004, pp. 24–45.

12 Anne H. Pinn and Anthony B. Pinn, *Fortress Introduction to Black Church History*, Minneapolis: Fortress Press, 2002, pp. 6–8.

13 David Ford, 'Theological Wisdom, British Style', *Christian Century* 117:11 (5 April 2000), pp. 388, 391; 'British Theology after

a Trauma: Divisions and Conversations', *Christian Century* 117:12 (12 April 2000), pp. 425–31 and 'British Theology: Movements and Churches', *Christian Century* 117:13 (19–26 April 2000), pp. 467–73.

14 David Ford and Rachel Muers, *The Modern Theologians: An Introduction to Christian Theology since 1918*, 3rd edn, London: Blackwell, 2005.

15 Only seven of these have been put together in this volume as three of our colleagues opted not to have their work included at this time.

16 Bill Ashcroft, Gareth Griffiths, Helen Tiffin, *The Postcolonial Studies Reader*, New York: Routledge, 1995.

17 The following works are helpful in giving an overview of the relationship between postcolonial criticism and biblical studies: R. S. Sugirtharajah, *The Bible and the Third World: Precolonial, Colonial and Postcolonial Encounters*, Cambridge: Cambridge University Press, 2001; R. S. Sugirtharajah, *Postcolonial Criticism and Biblical Interpretation*, Oxford: Oxford University Press, 2002; Laura Donaldson, Kwok Pui-lan (eds), *Postcolonialism, Feminism and Religious Discourse*, New York, London: Routledge, 2002; Musa Dube, *Postcolonial Feminist Interpretation of the Bible*, St Louis, Missouri: Chalice Press, 2000.

18 R. S. Sugirtharajah, *Postcolonial Reconfigurations: An Alternative Way of Reading the Bible and Doing Theology*, London: SCM Press, 2003, p. 4

19 Christopher Duraisingh, 'Towards a Postcolonial Re-Visioning of the Church's Faith, Witness and Communion', in Ian T. Douglas and Kwok Pui-lan (eds), *Beyond Colonial Anglicanism*, New York: Church Publishing, 2001, 337–67, p. 337.

20 R. S. Sugirtharajah, 'Complacencies and Cul-de-sacs: Christian Theologies and Colonialism', *Postcolonial Reconfiguration*, p. 143.

21 Stuart Hall, 'Cultural Identity and Diaspora' in Jonathan Rutherford (ed.), *Identity: Community, Culture, Difference*, London: Laurence and Wishart, 1990, pp. 222–37.

22 See note 2 above.

23 R. S. Sugirtharajah, 'Charting the Aftermath: A Review of Postcolonial Criticism', in R. S. Sugirtharajah (ed.), *The Postcolonial Biblical Reader*, Oxford: Blackwell Publishing, 2006, [pp. 7–32] p. 27.

24 See chapter 5 of Alistair Kee, *The Rise and Demise of Black Theology*, Aldershot: Ashgate, 2006.

25 Paul Gilroy, *There Ain't No Black in the Union Jack*, London: Hutchinson, 1987.

Notes

26 Callum Brown, *The Death of Christian Britain: Understanding Secularisation 1800–2000*, London: Routledge, 2001. See also Grace Davie, *Religion in Britain since 1945: Believing without Belonging*, Oxford: Blackwell, 1994.

27 Reddie, *Black Theology in Transatlantic Dialogue*.

28 Three of the papers presented at the conference were not made available for publication in this text. David Isiorho and Caroline Redfearn's essays were not presented on the day. These were added in order to fill the spaces vacated by those essays that were unavailable. Isiorho and Redfearn's essays were both presented at the monthly Black Theology in Britain, which meets on the last Thursday of the month at the Queens Foundation, in Birmingham, chaired by Dr Anthony Reddie. Isiorho's paper was presented on 23 February 2006. Redfearn's paper was presented on 30 March 2006. Both papers have been slightly modified as they were originally given as talks and were not intended, initially, for publication.

29 See chapter 5 of Reddie, *Black Theology in Transatlantic Dialogue* for a rationale for this approach.

30 See Anthony G. Reddie, *Dramatizing Theologies: A Participative Approach to Black God-Talk*, London: Equinox, 2006.

31 It is interesting to note that in both Mark Sturge's, *Look What the Lord Has Done!*, London: Scripture Union, 2005 and Joe D. Aldred, *Respect: Understanding Caribbean British Christianity*, Peterborough: Epworth, 2005, greater emphasis is given to Black British Pentecostalism as opposed to Black people in other churches. The normativity of this discourse belies the eclectic and plural nature of Black spirituality in Britain (for example, more Black people are sacramental as opposed to charismatic evangelical in Britain, in terms of spirituality and liturgical practices).

Chapter 1

1 Thomas Groome, *Sharing Faith*, San Francisco: Harper, 1991. See also N. Lynne Westfield, *Dear Sisters: A Womanist Practice of Hospitality*, Cleveland, Ohio: The Pilgrim Press, 2001. It is also worth noting Anne Hope and Sally Timmel, *Training for Transformation: A Handbook for Community Workers* – in four volumes, Gweru, Zimbabwe: Mambo Press, 1999.

2 Anthony B. Pinn, *Noise and Spirit: The Religious and Spiritual Sensibilities of Rap Music*, New York: New York University Press, 2003.

3 Michael Eric Dyson, *Between God and Gangsta Rap*, New York: Oxford University Press, 1996.

4 See Robert Beckford, *God of the Rahtid*, London: Darton, Longman & Todd, 2001.

5 Linda E. Thomas, 'Womanist Theology, Epistemology, and a New Anthropological Paradigm' in Linda E. Thomas (ed.) *Living Stones in the Household of God: The Legacy and Future of Black Theology*, Minneapolis: Fortress Press, 2003, pp. 37–50. See also pp. 107–15.

6 See M. Bulmer, *The Chicago School of Sociology*, Chicago: University of Chicago Press, 1984.

7 W. F. Whyte, *Learning from the Field: A Guide from Experience* (with the collaboration of Kathleen Whyte), London: Sage, 1984.

8 M. Hammersley, 'What's Wrong with Ethnography? The Myth of Theoretical Description', *Sociology* 24:4 (1990), pp. 597–615. *What's Wrong with Ethnography? Methodological Explorations*, London: Routledge, 1992; *Social Research: Philosophy, Politics and Practice*, London: Sage, 1993. M. Hammersely and P. Atkinson, *Ethnography: Principles in Practice*, London: Routledge, 1983.

9 B. Glaser and A. Strauss, *The Discovery of Grounded Theory*, Chicago: Aldine, 1967.

10 Ken Pryce, *Endless Pressure: A Study of West Indian Life Styles in Bristol*, Bristol: Bristol Classical Press, 1986.

11 A. Bryman, *Doing Research in Organisations*, London: Routledge, 1988.

12 D. Silverman, *Qualitative Methodology and Sociology*, Aldershot: Gower, 1985.

13 Michael Eric Dyson, *Reflecting Black: African-American Cultural Criticism*, Minneapolis: University of Minneapolis Press, 1993, pp. 221–330 for a good example of this kind of work. See also Robert Beckford, *Jesus Is Dread*, London: Darton, Longman & Todd, 1998.

14 'The Christian Education of African Caribbean Children in Birmingham: Creating a New Paradigm through Developing Better Praxis', unpublished PhD thesis, University of Birmingham, 2000.

15 See http://www.windbags.freeserve.co.uk for a brief description and analysis of Barn Dances.

16 Constraints of time and the scope of the project meant that I chose to work more extensively with this group, although I used the two other groups at other points in the research.

17 This was not a controlled, scientific piece of research (the group was not created to be a representation of a larger population in survey terms), so the responses should not be taken as empirical evidence.

18 See Anthony G. Reddie, *Nobodies to Somebodies*, Peterborough: Epworth Press, 2003, pp. 152–4. See also Anthony G. Reddie, 'Pentecost – Dreams and Visions (a Black theological reading)' in Maureen Edwards (ed.) *Discovering Christ: Ascension and Pentecost*, Birmingham: International Bible Reading Association, 2001, pp. 27–42.

19 See Jerome W. Berryman, *Godly Play: An Imaginative Approach to Religious Education*, Minneapolis: Augsburg, 1991.

20 N. Lynne Westfield, *Dear Sisters: A Womanist Practice of Hospitality*, Cleveland, Ohio: The Pilgrim Press, 2001.

21 Janice Hale-Benson, *Black Children: Their Roots, Culture, and Learning Styles*, Baltimore: The Johns Hopkins University Press, 1986.

22 Hale-Benson, *Black Children*, pp. 21–44.

23 Dwight N. Hopkins, 'Black Theology on Theological Education' in Dwight N. Hopkins (ed.), *Black Faith and Public Talk*, New York: Orbis Books, 1999, pp. 41–52.

24 Beckford, *God of the Rahtid*, p. 12.

25 See Frederick L. Ware, *Methodologies of Black Theology*, Cleveland, Ohio: The Pilgrim Press, 2002, pp. 115–44.

26 Theophus H. Smith, *Conjuring Culture: Biblical Formations of Black America*, New York: Oxford University Press, 1994, pp. 4–6.

27 Smith, *Conjuring Culture*, pp. 4–6

28 Ware, *Methodologies of Black Theology*, p. 135

29 Albert J. Raboteau, *Slave Religion*, New York: Oxford University Press, 1978.

30 Robert E. Hood, *Must God Remain Greek? Afro-Cultures and God-Talk*, Minneapolis: Fortress Press, 1990.

31 Cheryl Bridges Johns, *Pentecostal Formation: A Pedagogy among the Oppressed*, Sheffield: Sheffield Academic Press, 1998, pp. 62–137.

32 Robert Beckford, *Dread and Pentecostal*, London: SPCK, 2000, pp. 168–82.

33 Peter J. Paris, *The Spiritualities of African Peoples: The Search for a Common Moral Discourse*, Minneapolis: Fortress Press, 1995, pp. 27–57.

34 Brigid M. Sackey, 'Spiritual Deliverance as a Form of Health Delivery: A Case Study of the Solid Rock Chapel International', *Black Theology in Britain: A Journal of Contextual Praxis* 4:2 (May 2002), pp. 150–71.

35 Anthony G. Reddie, *Faith, Stories and the Experience of Black Elders*, London: Jessica Kingsley, 2001, pp. 106.

36 Christine Callender, *Education for Empowerment: The Practice and Philosophies of Black Teachers*, Stoke-on-Trent: Trentham Books, 1997, pp. 65–95.

37 See Anthony B. Pinn, *Terror and Triumph: The Nature of Black Religion*, Minneapolis: Fortress Press, 2003 and Patricia Hill Collins, *Black Feminist Thought: Knowledge, Consciousness and the Politics of Empowerment*, London: Routledge, 1990 as excellent examples for the kind of work I have in mind.

38 Reddie, *Nobodies to Somebodies*, pp. 97–9.

39 Reddie, *Nobodies to Somebodies*, pp. 97–8.

40 Reddie, *Faith, Stories and the Experience of Black Elders*, pp. 108–10, and Reddie, *Nobodies to Somebodies*, pp. 122–5.

41 An excellent example of this method can be found in Juan Luis Segundo, *The Liberation of Theology*, Maryknoll, New York: Orbis, 1976.

42 See Harry H. Singleton III, *Black Theology and Ideology: Deideological Dimensions in the Theology of James H. Cone*, Collegeville, Minnesota: The Liturgical Press, 2002.

43 See Robert Beckford, *God and the Gangs*, London: Darton, Longman & Todd, 2004.

44 Beckford, *God and the Gangs*, pp. 85–111.

45 See *Contact: Practical Theology and Pastoral Care* 146 (2005) for an entire issue dedicated to the role of theological reflection within practical theology.

Chapter 2

1 This was an attempt to adapt *Growing into Hope* by A. G. Reddie, Peterborough: Methodist Publishing House, 1998, originally created for Christian Education for use as a web-based religious education resource in schools (The Cream Project).

2 Eric E. Pemberton, 'A Study in Caribbean Religions', unpublished MPhil thesis, University of Birmingham, 1988.

3 Pemberton does not limit his focus to Christianity but incorporates the wider African and Caribbean religious experience, including African traditional religions, Islam and Hinduism.

4 V. Becher, *Black Christians: Black Church Traditions in Britain*, Birmingham: Centre for Black and White Christian Partnership and Westhill RE Centre, 1995.

5 The Agreed Syllabuses of Local Education Authorities such as Sandwell, Southwark, Lewisham and Leicester have, to varying degrees and in different ways, attempted to incorporate Black reli-

gious experience, such as including work on Black-led churches, Rastafarianism and African traditional religions, etc.

6 James H. Cone, *Black Theology and Black Power*, Maryknoll, New York: Orbis Books, 1997, p. 31 (originally published 1969).

7 James H. Cone, *A Black Theology of Liberation*, twentieth anniversary edition, Maryknoll, New York: Orbis, 1990, p. 6.

8 Dwight N. Hopkins, *Introducing Black Theology of Liberation*, New York: Orbis Books, 1999, p. 4.

9 That is to say, coming from a European or North American perspective but used as if it spoke for all.

10 This would cover ages 7 to approximately 12 years old.

11 This is not to say that this is entirely impossible within a non-confessional, educational environment. Rather, that such discussion would be more suitable for older age groups.

12 Frederick L. Ware, *Methodologies of Black Theology*, Cleveland, Ohio: The Pilgrim Press, 2002, pp. 66–114.

13 For example William R. Jones asks questions about the assumption of an all-powerful and loving God who is on the side of Black people, which appears to be contradicted by continued Black suffering. See Jones, *Is God a White Racist? A Preamble to Black Theology*, Boston: Beacon Press, 1998 originally published 1973.

14 Ware, *Methodologies of Black Theology*, p. 74.

15 Ware, *Methodologies of Black Theology*, p. 100.

16 Ware, *Methodologies of Black Theology*, p. 101, here referring to Cornel West.

17 B. Naidoo, 'To Confine or to Connect?' in A. Fyfe and P. Figueroa (eds), *Education for Cultural Diversity: The Challenge for a New Era*, London: Routledge, 1993, p. 260.

18 From 'Unit 4C: Why Is Easter Important for Christians?' on the DFES website at http://www.standards.dfes.gov.uk/schemes2/religion/rel4c/4cq5?view=get and http://www.standards.dfes.gov.uk/schemes2/religion/rel4c/4cq6?view=get (last accessed 9 February 2005). This is not to say that these points are not important but that other approaches to the subject may also be implemented.

19 From the *Jesus as Hope* lessons on the Cream Project website at: http://www.thecreamproject.org/. In this exercise, the young people are introduced to issues around poverty and hunger, deportation and displacement, and the right to speak out against injustice.

20 Found at: http://www.thecreamproject.org

21 Found at: http://www.thecreamproject.org

22 This stands for the Spiritual, Moral, Social and Cultural development of pupils, which is to be promoted through various curriculum subjects and also within the school ethos etc. See National

Curriculum Online, available at: www.nc.uk.net/nc_resources/html/ ks1and2.shtml (accessed 6 September 2004).

23 See National Curriculum Online (as above) under Learning across the National Curriculum: Promoting spiritual, moral, social and cultural development across the National Curriculum.

24 See National curriculum Online as above.

25 From National Curriculum Online. Available at: http://www. nc.uk.net. See under 'PSHE, Key Stage 2 – Knowledge, skills and understanding' (accessed 6 September 2004).

26 From National Curriculum Online. Available at: http://www. nc.uk.net. See under 'Citizenship, Key Stage 3 – Knowledge, skills and understanding' (accessed 6 September 2004).

27 This concern remains despite my recourse to the Black Philosophical School.

Chapter 3

1 Gospel music regularly appears on mainstream radio and television. It has also attracted mainstream media interest, for instance, in 2001 and 2003, the television production company GMTV, in association with *The Voice* newspaper, collaborated together in search of Britain's best gospel outfit. Television viewers were encouraged to place their vote for which artist/group they considered the best, and the winners won the coveted prize of a recording deal. Additionally, the newly formed Gospel Entertainment Music Awards (GEM awards), is a British gospel music awards ceremony that places emphasis on entertainment. In 2004, the BBC broadcast the event.

2 Paul Gilroy discusses Black artists, namely creators and producers of blues, gospel, soul and reggae, responding to a global audience. The creators of Black British gospel music are increasingly responding to a secular global audience. See Paul Gilroy, *There Ain't No Black in the Union Jack*, London: Routledge Classics, 1987, p. 206.

3 Black British theologian, Robert Beckford, *Jesus Is Dread: Black Theology and Black Culture in Britain*, London, Darton, Longman & Todd, 1998.

4 Kortright Davis, *Emancipation Still Comin': Explorations in Caribbean Emancipatory Theology*, New York: Orbis Books, 1990, p. 129.

5 Donnie McClurkin, *Live in London* (© and publishing rights Verity Music) 2001.

6 Beckford, *Jesus Is Dread*, p. 35.

Notes

7 See Cain Hope Felder, who explores biblical usage in American Black churches. Cain Hope Felder, *Troubling Biblical Waters*, New York: Orbis Books, 2002, p. 79.

8 Wendell Mapson, Jr, *The Ministry of Music in the Black Church*, Valley Forge: Judson Press, 1984, p. 39.

Chapter 4

1 V. Alexander, '"Breaking Every Fetter": To what Extent Has the Black-led Church in Britain Developed a Theology of Liberation?', unpublished PhD Thesis University of Warwick: Warwick, 1996, p. 22.

2 J. Harris, *Pastoral Theology: A Black-Church Perspective*, Minneapolis: Fortress Press, 1991, p. 11.

3 H. Marcuse, *One-Dimensional Man*, London: Routledge, 1964, p. 1.

4 R. Beckford, *Jesus Is Dread: Black Theology and Black Culture in Britain*, London: Darton, Longman & Todd, 1998.

5 N. Blaikie, *Approaches to Social Enquiry*, Cambridge: Polity Press, 1993.

6 R. Chrisman, 'Introduction' in R. Chrisman and N. Hare, *Contemporary Black Thought: The Best from the Black Scholar*, Indianapolis and New York: The Bobbs-Merrill Company, Inc., 1973, p. x.

7 R. Schreiter, 'Inculturation of Faith or Identification with Culture' in J. Scherer and S. Bevans, *New Directions in Mission and Evangelisation 3*, New York: Orbis Books, 1999.

8 E. Lartey, 'Editorial', in *Black Theology in Britain: A Journal of Contextual Praxis*, 1:1 (1998), pp. 7–9.

9 L. Cohn-Sherbok, 'Black Theology', in *Dictionary of Ethics, Theology and Society*, London and New York: Routledge, 1996, p. 80.

10 Lartey, 'Editorial'.

11 W. Jennings, 'Black Theology' in A. Hastings, *et al.* (eds), *The Oxford Companion to Christian Thought*, Oxford: Oxford University Press, 2000, p. 72.

12 S. Maimela, 'Black Theology', in K. Muller, *et al.* (eds), *Dictionary of Mission: Theology, History, Perspectives*, Maryknoll: New York 1997, p. 48.

13 E. Lartey, 'After Stephen Lawrence: Characteristics and Agenda for Black Theology in Britain', in *Black Theology in Britain: A Journal of Contextual Praxis*, 3 (1999), pp. 79–91.

14 Lartey, 'After Stephen Lawrence'.

Notes

15 P. Fryer, *Staying Power: The History of Black People in Britain*, London: Pluto Press, 1984; R. Ramdin, *The Making of the Black Working Class in Britain*, Aldershot: Gower, 1987.

16 *Black Community Report*, Vol. 1. London: Amenta Marketing Ltd, 1996; A. Trotman, 'Black, Black-led or What?' in Edwards, J. (ed.), *Let's Praise Him Again!* Eastbourne: Kingsway Publications, 1992.

17 Lartey, 'Editorial'.

18 J. Cone, *Black Theology and Black Power*, Minnesota: The Seabury Press, 1974, pp. 143–52.

19 M. Gergen and K. Gergen, *Social Construction: A Reader*, London: Sage Publications, 2003, p. 16.

20 M. Christian, *Black Identity in the 20th Century: Expressions of the US and UK African Diaspora*, London: Hansib, 2002, p. xvii.

21 R. Walker, *Classical Splendour Roots of Black History: A Comprehensive Guide to the Ancient and Mediaeval History of Africa*, London: Bogle-L'Ouverture Press, 1999, p. 14.

22 M. Jagessar, 'Review' in *Black Theology in Britain: A Journal of Contextual Praxis*, 4:2 (2002).

23 N. Pityana, 'Towards a Black Theology for Britain' in A. Havey (ed.), *Theology in the City: A Theological Response to Faith in the City*, London: SPCK, 1989.

24 Jagessar, 'Review'.

25 M. Sturge, *Look What the Lord Has Done: An Exploration of Black Christian Faith in Britain*, Blatchley: Scripture Union, 2005, p. 3.

26 H. Gouldbourne, (ed.) *Black Politics in Britain*, Aldershot: Avebury, 1990.

27 G. Carey, 'Evangelism', in A. Hastings, *et al.* (eds) *The Oxford Companion to Christian Thought*, Oxford: Oxford University Press, 2000, p. 221.

28 J. Aldred, 'A Black-Majority Church's Future', unpublished Masters Dissertation, University of Sheffield, 1994; Beckford, *Jesus Is Dread*; R. Beckford, *Dread and Pentecostal: A Political Theology for Black Pentecostal Churches in Britain*, London: SPCK, 2000.

29 M. Dixon, 'A Taste for Black Christians', *The Tablet* (16 February 2002), p. 25.

30 Aldred, 'A Black-Majority Church's Future', p. 2.

31 L. Dixon, 'A Reflection on Black Identity and Belonging in the Context of the Anglican Church in England: A Way Forward', *Black Theology in Britain: A Journal of Contextual Praxis*, 4 (2000), pp. 22–37; A. Reddie, 'The Christian Education of African-Caribbean Children in Birmingham: Creating a New Paradigm

through Developing Better Praxis', unpublished PhD thesis, University of Birmingham, 2000; A. Reddie, *Faith, Stories and the Experience of Black Elders: Singing the Lord's Song in a Strange Land*, London: Jessica Kingsley, 2001; A. Reddie, 'African-Centred Approaches to Education as a Resource for Christian Education' in *British Journal of Religious Education* 25:1 (2002); J. Wilkinson, *Church in Black and White: The Black Christian Tradition in 'Mainstream' Churches in England: A White Response*, Edinburgh: St Andrews Press, 1993.

32 J. Moltmann, *The Crucified God*, London: SCM Press, 1974, p. 1.

33 Moltman, *The Crucified God*.

34 www.ntcg.org.uk (27.04.05).

35 J. Aldred, 'Mission, Inculturation and Black Communities' in S. Barrow and G. Smith, *Christian Mission in Western Society*, London: Churches Together in Britain and Ireland, 2001, p. 179.

36 C. Anderson, 'Where there Is no Youth the Vision Will Perish' in *Black Theology in Britain: A Journal of Contextual Praxis* 6 (2001), pp. 25–39.

37 M. Simmonds, 'A Portrayal of the Life and Worship of the First United Church of Jesus Christ (Apostolic) UK', unpublished MA thesis, University of Birmingham, 1988, p. 45.

38 P. Mohabir, *Building Bridges*, London: Hodder & Stoughton, 1988, p. 84.

39 Alexander, "Breaking Every Fetter"; R. Beckford, 'Towards Post-colonial, Post-modern, Black Churches in Britain', in *Report of the Proceedings of the Consultation Between the World Council of Churches and African-Caribbean Church Leaders in Britain*, Geneva: World Council of Churches, 1995.

40 L. Williams, *Caribbean Theology*, New York: Peter Lang, 1994.

41 Schreiter, 'Inculturation of Faith or Identification With Culture'.

42 Schreiter, 'Inculturation', p. 75.

43 Payne, cited in Williams, *Caribbean Theology*, p. 151.

44 K. Coleman, 'Black to the Future: Re-Evaluating Black Youth', *Black Theology in Britain: A Journal of Contextual Praxis*, 6, (2001), pp. 41–51.

45 Coleman, 'Black to the Future'.

46 R. Nathan, 'Caribbean Youth Identity in the United Kingdom: A Call for a Pan-African Theology' in *Black Theology in Britain: A Journal of Contextual Praxis* 1 (1998), pp. 19–34.

47 Nathan, 'Caribbean Youth Identity', p. 27.

48 Nathan, 'Caribbean Youth Identity', p. 28.

49 Nathan, 'Caribbean Youth Identity', p. 29.

50 Nathan, 'Caribbean Youth Identity', p. 29.

51 Nathan, 'Caribbean Youth Identity', pp. 30–1.

52 R. Beckford, 'Prophet of Dub: Dub as a Heuristic for Theological Reflection' in *Black Theology in Britain: A Journal of Contextual Praxis* 1:1 (2002), pp. 67–82.

53 Beckford, *Jesus Is Dread*.

54 Beckford, 'Prophet of Dub', pp. 67–82.

55 J. Aldred, *Preaching with Power: Sermons by Black Preachers*, London: Cassell, 1998.

56 Beckford, *Dread and Pentecostal*, p. 197.

57 M. Karenga, *Introduction to Black Studies*, California: The University of Sankore Press, 1993, p. 311.

58 J. Aldred, 'Respect: A Caribbean British Theology', unpublished PhD thesis: University of Sheffield, 2003, p. 163.

59 Alexander, "Breaking Every Fetter", p. 212.

60 For further supporting evidence of preachers discussing sociopolitical issues from in the pulpit see Alexander, 'Breaking Every Fetter'; R. Gerloff, 'The African Diaspora in the Caribbean and Europe from Pre-emancipation to the Present Day', in *Cambridge History of Christianity*, 8 (2005), pp. 1–38 .

61 D. Muir, 'Black Theology, Pentecostalism and Racial Struggles in the Church of God', unpublished PhD thesis, King's College University of London, 2003, p. 85.

62 R. Nathan, 'Issues for the Black Minister' in P. Grant and R. Patel, *A Time to Speak: Perspective of Black Christian in Britain*. A Joint Publication Race Justice and the Black Theology Working Group, 1990, p. 13.

63 G. Parsons, 'Filling a Void? Afro-Caribbean Identity and Religion' in G. Parsons (ed.), *The Growth of Religious Diversity Britain from 1945*, Vol. 1 Traditions. London: Routledge, 1993; Trotman, 'Black, Black-led or What?'.

64 Sturge, *Look What the Lord Has Done*.

65 Muir, 'Black Theology', pp. 61–2.

66 R. Gerloff, *A Plea for Black British Theologies*, Frankfurt a.m and New York: Peter Lang, 1992.

67 Muir, 'Black Theology', p. 62.

68 Beckford, 'Prophet of Dub', pp. 67–82.

69 K. Owusu (ed.), *Black British Culture and Society: A Reader*, London: Routledge, 2000, p. 420.

70 Owusu, *Black British Culture*, p. 420.

71 Beckford, 'Prophet of Dub', pp. 67–82.

Notes

72 Beckford, 'Prophet of Dub'.

73 S. Arnold, *From Scepticism to Hope*, Nottingham: Grove Books Ltd, 1992; Parsons, 'Filling a Void?'; Gerloff, *A Plea for Black British Theologies*.

74 M. Phillips, 'A Faith in the Future?', *Time Out* 448 (17–23 November 1978), pp. 14–15.

75 Phillips, 'A Faith in the Future?', pp. 14–15.

76 Phillips, 'A Faith in the Future?', p. 15.

77 R. Mouw, 'Life in the Spirit in an Unjust World' in *PNEUMA* 9:2 (1987), 109–28, p. 77.

78 Mouw, 'Life in the Spirit', p. 117.

79 W. Hollenweger, *The Pentecostals*, London: SCM Press, 1972, p. 21.

80 R. Gerloff, Missionary from the Perspective of the Impoverished and Excluded, Ninth International Association for Mission Studies Conference, Buenos Aires, Argentina 10–19 April 1996, p. 9.

81 D. Nelson, 'For Such a Time like this: The Story of Bishop William J. Seymour and the Azusa Street Revival: A Search for Pentecostal/Charismatic Roots', unpublished PhD thesis, University of Birmingham, 1981, p. 15.

82 R. Beckford, 'Doing' Black Theology in the UK', in *Black Theology in Britain: A Journal of Contextual Praxis* 4 (2000), pp. 38–60.

83 R. Williams, *On Christian Theology*, Oxford: Blackwell, 2000, p. xiii.

84 R. Williams, *On Christian Theology*, p. xiv.

85 Louise Diamond cited by M. Abu-Nimer, 'Dialogue in the Second Intifada: Between Despair and Hope', *Global Dialogue* 4:2 (Summer 2003), p. 131.

86 P. Collins, *Black Feminist Thought: Knowledge, Consciousness and the Politics of Empowerment*, London: Routledge, 2000, p. 30.

87 Collins, *Black Feminist Thought*.

88 A. Pinn, *Why Lord? Suffering and Evil in Black Theology*, New York: Continuum, 1995, p. 20.

89 J. Cone, *For My People. Black Theology and the Black Church: Where Have We Been and Where Are We Going?*, Maryknoll: New York, 1984.

90 J. Roberts, *Black Theology in Dialogue*, Philadelphia: Westminster Press, 1987.

91 Williams, *On Christian Theology*, p. xiv.

92 Pinn, *Why Lord*.

93 Williams, *On Christian Theology*, p. xiv.

94 I. Brooks, *Another Gentleman to the Ministry*, Birmingham, Compeer Press Ltd (no date), p. 76.

95 Collins, *Black Feminist Thought*, p. 31.

96 N. Fairclough, *Discourse and Social Change*, Cambridge: Polity Press, 1992, p. 9.

97 K. Marx and F. Engels, *Selected Works*, Vol. 1, London: Lawrence and Wishart, 1968, p. 181.

98 Marx and Engels, *Selected Works*, Vol. 1, p. 30.

99 Reddie, *Faith, Stories and the Experience of Black Elders*.

100 Gerloff, 'The African Diaspora', p. 36.

101 A. Dorfman, 'The Lone Ranger, Barber and Other Innocent Heroes' in Gergen and Gergen, *Social Construction*, p. 201.

Chapter 5

1 Isaac Padinjarekuttu, *The Missionary Movement of Nineteenth and Twentieth Centuries and its Encounter with India*, Frankfurt: Peter Lang, 1995, p. 166.

2 Jeffrey Cox, *Imperial Fault Lines: Christianity and Colonial Power in India 1818–1940*, Stanford: Stanford University Press, 2002, p. 26.

3 G. Studdert-Kennedy, *Providence and the Raj: Imperial Mission and Missionary Imperialism*, New Delhi/London: Sage Publications, 1998, p. 29.

4 Edward Said, *Culture and Imperialism*, Chatto & Windus: London, 1993, p. 225.

5 D. Kooiman, *Conversion and Social Equality in India: The London Missionary Society in South Travencore in the Nineteenth Century*, Manohar Publications: New Delhi, 1989, p. 145.

6 www.missionstudies.org/asia/india (accessed 18 September 2006).

7 Jayakiren Sebastian, 'Pressure on the Hyphen: Aspects of the Search for Identity Today in Indian Christian Theology', *Religion and Society* 44 (1997), pp. 27–42.

8 R. S. Sugirtharajah, 'Imperial Critical Commentaries: Christian Discourse and Commentarial Writings in Colonial India', *Journal for the Study of the New Testament*, 73(1999), pp. 87–8.

9 Among the missionary attempts to interpret the Bible for the Indian Christians and clergy, the following are very significant: Verrier Elvin, *The Supremacy of the Spiritual*, Madras: CLSI, 1933; W. M. Stewart, *The Sacrament of Baptism*, Madras: CLSI, 1949; J.

Notes

R. Macphail, *The Jesus of History*, Madras: CLSI, 1933; Earlie
Albert Rowell, *God Speaks*, Poona: The Oriental Watchman
Publishing House, 1937.

10 R. S. Sugiratharajah, *Postcolonial Criticism and Biblical Interpretation*, Oxford: Oxford University Press, 2002, pp. 25–40.

11 F. F. Segovia and Stephen D. Moore (eds), *Postcolonial Biblical
Criticism: Interdisciplinary Intersections*, London: T&T Clark,
2005.

12 Segovia and Moore, *Postcolonial Biblical Criticism*, p. 75.

13 H. H. Esser, 'Grace, Spiritual Gifts', in *The New International
Dictionary of the New Testament Theology*, Vol. 2, ed. Colin Brown,
Exeter: The Paternoster Press, 1971, p. 115.

14 Esser, 'Grace, Spiritual Gifts', p. 117.

15 Leonardo Boff, *The Maternal Face of God*, San Francisco:
Harper & Row, 1979, p. 132.

16 Elsa Tamez, *Bible of the Oppressed*, Maryknoll: Orbis, 1982,
p. 72.

17 Leonardo Boff, *Liberating Grace*, Maryknoll: Orbis, 1981, pp.
163–74.

18 D. E. Nineham, *Saint Mark*, Harmondsworth: Penguin Books
1963, p. 150.

19 M. A. Reid, 'The Bible of the Frascados: Reading from the
Excluded', in M. A. Oduyoye and H. M. Vroom (eds), *One Gospel –
Many Cultures*, Amsterdam: WARC, 2003, p. 199.

20 Marion Grau, *Of Divine Economy: Refinancing Redemption*,
London: T&T Clark, 2004, p. 56.

Chapter 6

1 See P. Wright, *On Living in an Old Country*, London: Verso,
1985.

Chapter 7

1 Mary Waters, *Black Identities: West Indian Immigrants
Dreams and American Realities*, MA: Harvard University Press,
1999, pp. 19–43. For an excellent examination of the formation of
the Pan-Caribbean identity, see Franklin W. Knight, 'Migration, the
Plantation Society and the Emergence of a Pan-Caribbean Culture',
in *Caribbean Migration Program*, Gainesville: Center for Latin
American Studies, University of Florida, 1982.

Notes

2 Stuart Hall, *Myths of Caribbean Identity*, The Walter Rodney Memorial Lecture, UK, University of Warwick, 1991, p. 1.

3 R. S. Sugirtharajah, *Postcolonial Criticism and Biblical Interpretation*, Oxford: Oxford University Press, 2002, p. 181.

4 Sugirtharajah, *Postcolonial Criticism*, pp. 182–3.

5 Sugirtharajah, *Postcolonial Criticism*, p. 183.

6 Sugirtharajah, *Postcolonial Criticism*, p. 183.

7 Sugirtharajah, *Postcolonial Criticism*, p. 183.

8 Joseph M. Murphy, *Working the Spirit: Ceremonies of the African Diaspora*, MA: Beacon Press, 1994, pp. 178–9.

9 Khachig Tololyan, 'The Nation State and its Others: In Lieu of a Preface', *Diaspora* 1:1 (1991), pp. 4–5.

10 William Saffran, 'Diasporas in Modern Societies: Myths of Homeland and Return', *Diaspora*, 1:1 (1991), pp. 83–99.

11 Saffran, 'Diasporas in Modern Societies', p. 94.

12 Robin Cohen, *Global Diaspora: Introduction*, London: UCL Press, 1997, pp. 22–6.

13 Cohen, *Global Diaspora*, pp. 22–6.

14 Cohen, *Global Diaspora*, p. 180.

15 George Lamming, *Pleasures of Exile*, Michigan: University of Michigan Press, 1992, p. 56.

16 Lamming, *Pleasures of Exile*, p. 24.

17 Robert Beckford, *Dread and Pentecostal: A Political Theology for the Black Church in Britain*, London: SPCK, 2000, pp. 8–9.

18 Beckford, *Dread and Pentecostal*, p. 9.

19 Beckford, *Dread and Pentecostal*, pp. 9–18.

20 Waters, *Black Identities*, p. 6.

21 Waters, *Black Identities*, pp. 6–7. For a study on the peculiarities of the Caribbean diasporan people, although the concern is about their predisposition to political involvement, see Winston James, *Holding Aloft the Banner of Ethiopia: Caribbean Radicalism in America 1900–32*, London: Verso, 1998, pp. 50–91.

22 Waters, *Black Identities*, pp. 7–8. These can be described as the Caribbean diaspora moral values and ethics. However, they can become too individualistic and achievement-oriented. Seen within its context, these values are not only organic to the Caribbean experience but counter to Euro-American, even African-American moral values.

23 Milton Vickerman, *Crosscurrent: West Indian Immigrants and Race*, New York: Oxford University Press, 1999, p. 12. The Jamaican motto 'Out of Many, One People' makes it very easy to foster kinship with fellow Caribbeaners.

24 Vickerman, *Crosscurrent*, p. 11.

Notes

25 Vickerman, *Crosscurrent*, p. 11.

26 Vickerman, *Crosscurrent*, p. 11. For a discussion on the nature of the Caribbean diasporan life, see Virginia R. Dominguez, *From Neighbor to Stranger: The Caribbean Peoples in the United States*, CT: Antilles Research Program, Yale University, 1975. Barry Levine (ed.), *The Caribbean Exodus*, New York: Praeger Publishers, 1987; Ransford Palmer, *In Search of a Better life: Perspective on Migration from the Caribbean*, New York: Praeger Publishers, 1990; Constance Sutton 'Transnational Identities and Cultures: Caribbean Immigrants', in Michael D' Innocenzo and Josef P. Sirefman (eds), *The United States' Immigration and Ethnicity: American Society – 'Melting Pot' or 'Salad Bowl'*, CT: Greenwood Press, 1992; Nancy Foner (ed.), *New Immigrants in New York*, New York: Columbia University Press, 1987; and *Island in the Sun*, NY: Columbia University Press, 2001.

27 Vickerman, *Crosscurrent*, p. 26. A number of scholars have written about the experience of Caribbean people in the American experience with reference to the relationship to African-Americans. Interestingly, the relationship has not changed after more than fifty years since the earliest study was done. For an exploration of this issue, see Ira Reid, *The Negro Immigrant*, New York: Columbia University Press, 1939. Noteworthy are Lennox Raphael, 'West Indians and Afro-Americans', *Freedomways*, Summer 1964, pp. 438–45; Roy S. Bryce-Laporte, 'Black Immigrants, the Experience of Invisibility and Inequality', *Journal of Black Studies*, 3:1 (1972), pp. 29–56. Philip Kasinitz, 'The Minority Within: The New York Black Immigrants', *New York Affairs*, 10:1 (Winter 1987), pp. 44–58.

28 Vickerman, *Crosscurrent*, pp. 36–9. For further discussion on the origin of race and its relationship with ethnicity, see Mervyn C. Aleyne, *The Construction and Representation of Race and Ethnicity in the Caribbean and the World*, Kingston: University of the West Indies Press, 2002; David Baronov and Kevin A. Yelvongton, 'Ethnicity, Race Class, and Nationality Across the Caribbean', in Richard S. Hillman and Thomas J. D'Agostino (eds), *Understanding The Contemporary Caribbean*, Kingston: Ian Randle Publishers, 2003, pp. 209–32.

29 David Baronov and Kevin Yelivington, 'Ethnicity, Race, Class, and Nationality', in *Understanding the Contemporary Caribbean*, p. 221.

30 Reuel Rogers, "Black Like Who?' Afro-Caribbean Immigrants, African Americans, and the Politics of Group Identity', *Island in the City: West Indian Migration to New York*, Nancy Foner (ed.), Berkeley: University of California Press, 2001, p. 181.

31 Vickerman, *Crosscurrent*, p. 139.

32 Vickerman, *Crosscurrent*, p. 139.

33 Vickerman, *Crosscurrent*, pp. 137–60. The complex and disturbing relationship between the Caribbeans and African Americans cannot be examined in this study. Considerable study has been done over time: Reid, *The Negro Immigrant*; McKay, *Home to Harlem*, Boston: Northeastern University Press, 1987; Lennox Raphael, 'West Indians and African Americans', *Freedomways* 4:3 (Summer 1964), pp. 438–45; Orde Coombs, 'West Indians in New York: Moving Beyond the Limbo Pole', *New York Magazine* (July 13, 1970), pp. 28–32; Heather Hathaway, *Caribbean Waves: Relocating Claude McKay and Paule Marshall*, Bloomington: Indiana University Press, 1999.

34 Cornel West, *Race Matters*, Boston: Beacon Press, 1993, p. x.

35 Waters, *Black Identities*, p. 340.

36 Vickerman, *Crosscurrent*, p. 92. For an examination of how Caribbean people deal with racism, see Winston James, *Holding Aloft the Banner of Ethiopia: Caribbean Radicalism in America 1900–32*, New York: Verso Press, 1988, pp. 92–121; Waters, *Black Identities*, pp. 140–91.

37 Winston James and Clive Harris (eds), *Inside Babylon: The Caribbean Diaspora in Britain*, London: Verso Press, 1983, p. 233.

38 James and Harris, *Inside Babylon*, p. 243.

39 James and Harris, *Inside Babylon*, pp. 233–4.

40 G. Lewis, 'Race Relations in Britain: A View from the Caribbean', *Race Today* 1:3 (July 1969), p. 80. See also James and Harris, *Inside Babylon*, p. 234. They borrow the term 'Babylon' and find it pertinent to describe this racist ideology.

41 Emile Townes, *In a Blaze of Glory: Womanist Spirituality as Social Witness*, Nashville: Abingdon, 1995, p. 101.

42 Kortright Davis, *Emancipation Still Comin': Explorations in Caribbean Emancipatory Theology*, New York: Orbis Books, 1990, p. 24.

43 Towns, *In a Blaze of Glory*, p. 101.

44 Davis, *Emancipation Still Comin'*, p. 24.

45 James and Harris, *Inside Babylon*, p. 235.

46 Vickerman, *Crosscurrent*, pp. 92–4.

47 Vickerman, *Crosscurrent*, pp. 98–112.

48 Vickerman, *Crosscurrent*, p. 112. See also Waters, *Black Identities*.

49 Vickerman, *Crosscurrent*, p. 141. These are great virtues but they are individual interest. As they are practices by the Caribbean diaspora, they are not practised as communal ethics. For a study on

Notes

Black ethics, see Peter Paris, *The Spirituality of African Peoples: The Search for a Common Moral Discourse*, Minneapolis: Augsburg Fortress Press, 1995; Theodore Walker Jr, *Empower the People: Social Ethics for the African American Church*, New York: Orbis, 1991; Cheryl L. Sanders, *Empowerment Ethics for a Liberated People: A Path to African American Social Transformation*, Minneapolis: Fortress Press, 1995; Joan Martin, *More than Chains and Toil: A Christian Work Ethic of Enslaved Women*, Louisville, KY: Westminster John Knox Press, 2000. If Caribbean intellectual thought is to be authentically Caribbean, it must be rooted in its heritage. In the Black religious tradition, the pursuit of life was always for the common good. For a detailed study, see Winston Lawson, *Religion and Race*, New York: Peter Lang, 1996; Albert Raboteau, *Slave Religion*, New York: Oxford University Press, 1978. It is important that he specifically notes the African origin of the practice and how it informed the total life of the community.

50 Paris, *Spirituality of African Peoples*, p. 51. Although Paris clams to be writing a social ethic for the Black diaspora, the study is more about African-Americans. Taking his intent to be expressed in the title of the book, it is a spirituality for African peoples which includes the Caribbean diaspora. Even if it were for and about African-Americans, the work would still be relevant to the Caribbean diaspora.

51 Cornel West, *Prophesy Deliverance: An Afro-American Revolutionary Christianity*, Philadelphia: Westminster Press, 1982, p. 17. It is unfortunate that there has not been much thought on individualism in Black religious and theological thought. It is only recently that Black theologians have been addressing this as a theological issue but it is more a reactive attempt rather than a proactive intellectual pursuit. For example, *The Jordon Generation*, engages in this discussion as a critique to the apparently insidious sanitizing of individualism in contemporary Black religious and theological thought as represented in the works of Victor Anderson's *Beyond Ontological Blackness: An Essay on African American Religious and Cultural Criticism*, New York: Continuum, 1995. The roots of individualism are in the Enlightenment and Protestant theology. Its justification is in the American Constitution and the United Nations Document on Human Rights. This, however, does not mean an uncritical acceptance. In fact, this issue and practice need to be interpreted in light of the gospel of Jesus Christ. This issue is characteristic of contemporary society especially in Black Christianity. See also Dale Andrews, *Practical Theology for Black Churches: Bridging Black Theology and African Folk Religion*, Louisville: Westminster

John Knox Press, 2002, pp. 67–88. For a discussion from a Caribbean perspective, see Burchell Taylor, *Free for All*, Kingston: Grace Foundation, 1991.

52 Paris, *Spirituality of African Peoples*, p. 117.

53 Paris, *Spirituality of African Peoples*, p. 118. Paris calls for individuals and communities to work together to achieve Black liberation. The cause is bigger and greater than any one person. Paris is speaking, however, of the African-American pursuit for justice. This call must be connected to the Black struggle for justice if it is truly about and for African peoples. For a fuller examination of this issue, see Amy Jacques Garvey, *Garvey and Garveyism*, New York: Macmillan Press, 1970; Rupert Lewis, *Marcus Garvey: Anti-Colonial Champion*, London: Karia Press, 1987; John Henrik Clark (ed.), *Marcus Garvey and the Vision of Africa*, New York: Vintage Books, 1974.

54 Sam Selvon, *Lonely Londoners*, New York: Longman Publishing Group, 1994, p. 138.

55 James and Harris, *Inside Babylon*, p. 255.

56 Rex Nettleford, *Inward Stretch, Outward Reach: A Voice from the Caribbean*, London: Macmillan Press, 1993, p. 173.

57 James and Harris, *Inside Babylon*, p. 255.

58 George Lamming, *The Emigrants*, London: Allison and Busby, 1990.

59 Oscar L. Bolioli (ed.), *The Caribbean: Culture of Resistance, Spirit of Hope*, New York: Friendship Press, 1993, p. 56. The Verdun Proclamation is the proceeding of the consultation sponsored by the Caribbean/African-American (CAAD) and the Caribbean Conference of Churches (CCC) held in Verdun, Barbados, 1–3 May 1992. The representatives of the event were from the Caribbean, North America and the United Kingdom. It was not only an ecumenical reflection on the issue of racism. The purpose of the event was an attempt to implement the decisions of the First Inter-Continental Consultation of Indigenous and Peoples of African Decent on racism. I find it interesting that this event took place without the inclusion and involvement of the people of the Caribbean diaspora. It is significant, however, that such an event occurred. It symbolizes the recognition of the particularity of ethnicity as well as the diversity of the Black race. Beyond that, it is a historic effort to address the common issue of racism. Racism affects all peoples but Black people, regardless of their ethnicity and location, are its victims. This was also an effort to cultivate relationships among the various Black communities. For an exposition on Jesus Christ as emancipator, see James H. Evans, *We Have Been Believers*,

Notes

Minneapolis: Fortress Press, 1992, pp. 77–98; Kortright Davis, 'Jesus Christ and Black Liberation', *Journal of Religious Thought* 42:1 (Summer–Fall 1985), pp. 51–67.

60 John S. Mbiti, *African Religions and Philosophy*, New York: Doubleday, 1970, p. 3. The role of faith, while central in Caribbean diasporan Christianity, must be considered in light of its African roots. For examination of this issue, see Winston Lawson, *Religion and Race: African and European Roots in Conflict – A Jamaican Testament*, New York: Peter Lang, 1996. For a fascinating study, see Mervyn Alleyne, *Roots of Jamaican Culture*, London: Pluto Press, 1988. The classic study on the subject is Albert Raboteau, *Slave Religion: The 'Invisible' in the Antebellum South*, New York: Oxford University Press, 1978. For a significant theological treatment of this subject, especially chapters 2 and 3, see J. Deotis Roberts, *Black Theology in Dialogue*, Philadelphia: Westminster John Knox Press, 1987.

61 The incarnation of Jesus Christ is not the subject of this study. It is important to note, however, that this is one of the most significant doctrines, even the core, of the Christian faith. It is the basis of the revelation of the humanity of God and God's presence in human history. This belief was affirmed in the first ecumenical council of the Church held in Nicea in 325 where the Nicene Creed was formulated and adopted. There was an attempt both to combat the Arian controversy and to have a commonly held set of doctrines that expresses the one faith. See Eusebius of Caesarea, *Life of Constantine*. One of the most prominent, if not the most prominent church thinker regarding the doctrine of the incarnation was Athanasius of Alexandria. He was highly revered and known as the 'Black Dwarf'. See his most significant writing on the doctrine of the incarnation, *On the Incarnation*, New York: St Vladimir's Orthodox Theological Seminary, 1989; 'Discourses against the Arians' in Philip Schaff and Henry Wace (eds), *The Nicene and Post Nicene Fathers*, Vol. IV, Michigan: Eerdmans, 1957. For study on the incarnation as it is understood in Black theology consult Howard Thurman, *Jesus and the Disinherited*, Nashville: Abingdon Press, 1949; George Kesley, *Racism and the Christian Understanding of Man*, New York: Charles Scribner's and Sons, 1965; Evans, *We Have Been Believers*.

62 Gayraud Wilmore, *Black and Presbyterian: Heritage and Hope*, Philadelphia: Westminster John Knox Press, 1983. The ethnicity of Jesus is a very controversial issue. There are two schools of thought on this issue, the literal and the existential. The former supports the idea that Jesus was literally a Black person. The major representative of the school is Albert Cleage Jr as delineated in his

classic work, *The Black Messiah*, Kansas: Sheed and Ward Inc., 1968; see also his *Black Christian Nationalism: New Directions for the Black Church*, New York: Marrow Quill, 1992; The latter view advocates the idea that Jesus was existentially Black. For further examination see James Cone, *God of the Oppressed*, New York: Seabury Press, 1995; Jacqueline Grant, *White Women's Christ and Black Women's Jesus: Feminist Christology and Womanist Response*, Atlanta: Scholars Press, 1998; see also her 'Black Christology: Interpreting Aspects of The Apostolic Faith', in David T. Shannon and Gayraud S. Wilmore (eds), *Black Witness to the Apostolic Faith*, Michigan: Eerdmans, 1985; Kelly Brown Douglas, *The Black Christ*, New York: Orbis Books, 1995; Kenneth L. Waters Sr, *Afrocentric Sermons: The Beauty of Blackness in the Bible*, Valley Forge: Judson Press, 1993. Tom Skinner, *How Black Is the Gospel*, New York: J. B. Lippincott, 1970; Randall Bailey and Jacquelyn Grant (eds), *The Recovery of the Black Presence: An Interdisciplinary Exploration*, Nashville: Abingdon Press, 1975; Ashley Smith, 'The Religious Significance of Black Power in Caribbean Churches', in Idris Hamid (ed.), *Troubling of the Waters*, Trinidad: Rahaman Printery Ltd, 1973, pp. 83–103; Earl August, 'The Spiritual Significance of Black Power', in Hamid, *Troubling of the Waters*, pp. 109–13.

63 F. F. Bruce, *The Acts of the Apostles*, Michigan: Eerdmans, 1965, pp. 53–64. Bible scholars do not agree about this notion of diversity. One school of thought teaches that these were not diaspora Jews but those who lived in Jerusalem. For a further examination, see E. Earnest Haenchen, *The Acts of the Apostles*, Philadelphia: Westminster John Knox Press, 1971, pp. 161–78.

64 William H. Willimon, 'Acts' in James L. Mays (ed.), *Interpretation Bible Commentary*, Atlanta: John Knox Press, 1988, pp. 27–8. Willimon agrees that Pentecost is the birth of the Church but thinks that it is more accurate to attribute it to Easter which is also the birth of Pentecost. Interestingly, he addresses the issue of the formation of the Church without considering its diversity. For a study on this issue, see Justo Gonzalez, *Acts: The Gospel of the Spirit*, New York: Orbis Books, 2001, pp. 33–48.

65 David Rhoads, *The Challenge of Diversity: The Witness of Paul and the Gospel*, Minneapolis: Fortress Press, 1996, p. 15; see also his, *From Every People and Nation*, Minneapolis: Fortress Press, 2005; James Dunn, *Unity and Diversity in the New Testament: An Inquiry into the Character of Earliest Christianity*, 2nd edn Philadelphia: Trinity Press International, 1990; Justo Gonzalez (ed.), *Out of Every Tribe and Nation*, Nashville: Abingdon, 1992; *The Acts of the Spirit*, New York: Orbis Books, 2001, pp. 33–7; Steven

McKenzie, *All God's Children*, KY: Westminster John Knox Press, 1997; Joel Edwards, *Lord, Make us One: Seeking Unity in Diversity*, London: Hodder & Stoughton, 1999; David T. Shannon and Gayraud S. Wilmore, *Black Witness to the Apostolic Faith*, Michigan: Eerdmans, 1985.

66 The origin of this term is unknown. It is commonly used in ordinary conversations especially during times of celebration and crises among Caribbean people to express their unity.

67 This is among the national symbols of Jamaica and is an expression that shapes its national identity being a country of diverse people groups. The motto is printed on Jamaican currency notes.

68 Amy J. Garvey, *Philosophy and Opinion of Marcus Garvey*, New York: Atheneum, 1986, 2 vols.

Chapter 8

1 This chapter will not include traditional biblical interpretation, though this will be a significant area of my research.

2 William Stewart, *Cassell's Queer Companion: A Dictionary of Lesbian and Gay Life and Culture*, London and New York: Cassell, 1995, p. 121.

3 Kelly Brown Douglas, *Sexuality and the Black Church: A Womanist Perspective*, Maryknoll, NY: Orbis, 1999, p. 6.

4 Carolyn Cooper, *Sound Clash: Jamaican Dancehall Culture at Large*, New York and London: Palgrave Macmillan, 2004, p. 162.

5 Alexa Hepburn, *An Introduction to Critical Psychology*, London: Sage Publications, 2004, p. 107.

6 Douglas, *Sexuality and the Black Church*, p. 6

7 Elias Farajaje-Jones 'Breaking Silence: Toward an In-the-Life Theology' in G. S. Wilmore and J. H. Cone (eds) *Black Theology: A Documentary History, 1966–1979*, Maryknoll, NY: Orbis, 1993, pp. 139–59.

8 Stewart, *Cassell's Queer Companion*, p. 122.

9 John Boswell, *Christianity, Social Tolerance and Homosexuality*, Chicago and London: University of Chicago Press, 1980, p. 44.

10 Vanessa Baird, *The No-Nonsense Guide to Sexual Diversity*, London: Verso/NIP, 2001, p. 29.

11 Farajaje-Jones, 'Breaking Silence', pp. 139–59.

12 Farajaje-Jones, 'Breaking Silence', p. 140.

13 Farajaje-Jones, 'Breaking Silence', p. 140.

14 Mark Jordon, *The Invention of Sodomy in Christian Theology*, Chicago and London: University of Chicago Press, 1997, p. 17.

15 Cooper, *Sound Clash*, p. 166.

16 See Martti Nissinen, *Homoeroticism in the Biblical World: A Historical Perspective*, Minneapolis, Fortress Press, 1998.

17 Tom Betteridge (ed.), *Sodomy in Early Modern Europe* Manchester: Manchester University Press, 2002, p. 1.

18 Sarah Salih, 'Sexual Identities: A Medieval Perspective' in Betteridge, *Sodomy in Early Modern Europe*, p. 113.

19 Salih, 'Sexual Identities', p. 116

20 Jordon, *Invention of Sodomy*, p. 18.

21 B. R. Burg, *Sodomy and the Pirate Tradition: English Sea Rovers in the Seventeenth Century Caribbean*, New York and London: New York University Press, 1984, p. xi.

22 Burg, *Sodomy and the Pirate Tradition*, p. xii.

23 Burg, *Sodomy and the Pirate Tradition*, p. xii.

24 This term, which in common parlance in African American popular culture refers to Black men who self-identify as heterosexual who, nevertheless, have sex with other men often in a covert manner – hence the term 'on the down-low'.

25 Baird, *No-Nonsense Guide*, p. 57.

26 Elizabeth Crespo-Kebler, 'The Infamous Crime against Nature' Constructions of Heterosexuality and Lesbian Subversions', in Lewis Linden (ed.), *The Culture of Gender and Sexuality in the Caribbean*, Gainesville, Tallahassee: University Press of Florida, 2003, pp. 190–211.

27 My definition of the 'Black church' for the sake of brevity refers to people of African-Caribbean descent who identify as Black and Christian within churches (Black majority, Black-led or otherwise), religious organizations and theologians within academia. This does not exclude an understanding of similar issues within the Muslim community, nor those on the margins of Black church life, nor within 'virtual' domains in cyberspace. In my section on the movement towards inclusivity I shall explore these nomenclatures.

28 Marrieta Morrissey, *Slave Women in the New World: Gender Stratification in the Caribbean*, Kansas: University Press of Kansas, 1989, p. 4.

29 Morrissey, *Slave Women in the New World*, p. 36.

30 Orlando Patterson, *The Sociology of Slavery: An Analysis of the Origins, Development and Structure of Negro Slave Society in Jamaica*, London: Cox & Wyman, 1967, pp. 40–1.

31 Patterson, *Sociology of Slavery*, p. 42 (my emphasis).

32 Patterson, *Sociology of Slavery*, p. 42.

33 Morrissey, *Slave Women in the New World*, p. 156.

34 Richard Dunn, *Sugar and Slaves: The Rise of the Planter Class*

in the English West Indies 1624–1713, London: Jonathan Cape, 1973, p. 224.

35 James Walvin, *Black Ivory*, 2nd edn, London: Fontana Press, 2001, p. 213.

36 Walvin, *Black Ivory*, p. 159 (my emphasis).

37 Walvin, *Black Ivory*, p. 110.

38 Walvin, *Black Ivory*, p. 115.

39 Walvin, *Black Ivory*, p. 146.

40 Walvin, *Black Ivory*, pp. 186–7.

41 Morrissey, *Slave Women in the New World*, p. 146

42 Orlando Patterson, *Rituals of Blood: Consequences of Slavery in Two American Centuries*, New York: Basic Civitas Books 1988, p. 289.

43 Patterson, *Rituals of Blood*, p. 289.

44 O'Brien Dennis, *The Cries of Men: Voices of Jamaican Men who have been Raped and Sexually Abused*, New York, Lincoln, Shanghai: iUniverse, Inc., 2005, p. 3.

45 Dennis, *Cries of Men*, p. 4

46 Horace Griffin, 'Their Own Received Them Not: African American Lesbians and Gays in Black Communities' in Elizabeth Stuart, Heather Walton and Gerard Loughlin (eds), *Theology and Sexuality: The Journal of the Centre for the Study of Christianity and Sexuality*, 12 (March 2000), pp. 88–100.

47 Baird, *No-Nonsense Guide*, pp. 58–9.

48 Tim Hitchcock, *English Sexualities 1700–1800*, London: Macmillan Press, 1997, p. 2.

49 Hitchcock, *English Sexualities*, p. 4.

50 Hitchcock, *English Sexualities*, p. 45.

51 Hitchcock, *English Sexualities*, p. 52.

52 Hitchcock, *English Sexualities*, p. 58.

53 Hitchcock, *English Sexualities*, p. 67.

54 Hitchcock, *English Sexualities*, p. 70.

55 Walvin, *Black Ivory*, p. 50

56 Walvin, *Black Ivory*, p. 213.

57 Joseph Dorsey, 'It Hurt very much at the Time: Patriarchy, Rape Culture, and Slave Body-Semiotic' in Linden, *Culture of Gender and Sexuality*, pp. 295–322 (p. 295).

58 Larry Gragg, *Englishmen Transplanted: The English Colonization of Barbados 1627–1660*, Oxford: Oxford University Press, 2003, p. 168.

59 Oliver Ransford, *The Slave Trade: The Story of the Transatlantic Slavery*, London: Cox & Wyman, 1971, p. 113.

60 Burg, *Sodomy and the Pirate Tradition*, p. xvi.

Notes

61 Burg, *Sodomy and the Pirate Tradition*, p. xvii.

62 Burg, *Sodomy and the Pirate Tradition*, p. 119.

63 Robert Aldrich, *Colonialism and Homosexuality*, London: Routledge, 2003, p. 2.

64 Burg, *Sodomy and the Pirate Tradition*, p. 3.

65 Burg, *Sodomy and the Pirate Tradition*, preface.

66 Mike Dyson, *The Michael Eric Dyson Reader*, New York: Basic Civitas Books, 2004, p. 238.

67 Griffin, 'Their Own Received Them Not', p. 93.

68 Kelly Brown Douglas, *Sexuality and the Black Church*, p. 84.

69 Kwok Pui-Lan, *Postcolonial Imagination and Feminist Theology*, London: SCM Press, 2004, pp. 188–9.

Chapter 9

1 Cf. David Buttrick, *Homiletic: Moves and Structures*, Philadelphia: Fortress Press, 1987, p. 41.

2 Philip Potter as quoted by Michael Jagessar in *Full Life for All: The Work and Theology of Philip A. Potter*, Zoetermeer: Boekencentrum, 1997, p. 127.

3 See James W. Boyd, 'Teaching the Diversity of World Religions', in William M. Timpson, Silvia Sara Canetto, Evelinn Borrayo and Raymond Yang (eds), *Teaching Diversity: Challenges and Complexities, Identities and Integrity*, Madison, WI: Atwood Publishing, 2003, pp. 65–76. I would concede, however, that in the interest of scholarship and research, my writing ought to reflect a 'fair' and 'even-handed' approach to the sources and subjects with which I am working.

4 Cf. Ada María Isasi-Díaz, *La Lucha Continues: Mujerista Theology*, Maryknoll: Orbis, 2004, pp. 50–4.

5 David Tracy, *Plurality and Ambiguity*, San Francisco: Harper & Row, 1987, p. 79.

6 Elsa Tamez, 'Reading the Bible under a Sky without Stars' in Walter Dietrich and Ulrich Luz (eds), *The Bible in a World Context: An Experiment in Contextual Hermeneutics*, Grand Rapids, Michigan/Cambridge, UK: Eerdmans, 2002, pp. 3–15.

7 I use the term 'Black' as a political (rather than cultural) construct to describe the racial identity of all Afro/Indo/Chinese Caribbean, Africans, Asians, etc.

8 Cleophus LaRue, *The Heart of Black Preaching*, Louisville, Kentucky: WJK Press, 2000, p. 2.

9 John Agard, 'The Coin of Birth' in *Weblines*, Newcastle upon

Tyne: Bloodaxe Books, 2000, p. 16.

10 The notion of Caribbean diaspora needs clarifying, given the complex nature of the pluralism inherent in the very notion. While the Caribbean itself is made up of diasporic peoples (from Africa, Asia and Europe) through forced migration (colonialism), my use of Caribbean diaspora is in the specific context of the Caribbean dispersals around the North Atlantic. Harry Goulbourne and John Solomos raise the question whether 'it is sensible to speak about a Caribbean diaspora or to speak of the Caribbean as a region in which a number of diasporas meet and clash, as social, and cultural plurality theory would suggest'. They suggest that any notion of a Caribbean diaspora 'must profoundly embrace the following factors: diversity (racial, ethnic, geographical, etc.); the region as the crossroads of the Americas; situated between developed industrialized and developing societies; and small physical spaces and populations but enjoying large cultural and physical dispersals around the North Atlantic world.' My use of the Caribbean and Caribbean diaspora broadly concurs with this understanding. 'The Caribbean Diaspora: Some Introductory Remarks', in *Ethnic and Racial Studies*, 27:4 (July 2004), pp. 533–43.

11 Gloria Anzaldúa, *Borderlands/La Frontera: The New Mestiza*, San Francisco: Spinsters/Aunt Lute, 1987, p. 23.

12 Wilson Harris, 'The Making of Tradition', in *Explorations*, Sydney: Dangaroo Press, 1981, pp. 88–96. See also 'Literacy and the Imagination – a Talk', in Michael Gilkes (ed.), *The Literate Imagination: Essays on the Novels of Wilson Harris*, London: Macmillan Caribbean, 1989, p. 29.

13 A. K. Ramanujan, 'Three Hundred Ramayanas: Five Examples and Three Thoughts on Translation', in Paul Richman (ed.), *Many Ramanayans: The Diversity of Traditions in South Asia*, Berkeley: University of California Press, 1991, p. 46.

14 Joan Aitchison, *The Language Web: The Power and Problem of Words*, Cambridge: Cambridge University Press, 1997, p. 95.

15 Frank J. Korom, *Hosay Trinidad: Muhuarram Performances in an Indo-Caribbean Diaspora*, Philadelphia: University of Pennsylvania Press, 2003. Korom suggests 'cultural creolization' as an alternative to the problematic notion of syncretism. He writes that creolization and related notion of decreolization 'allows me to emphasize the human agency, the conscious decisions made by human actors' in negotiating rituals on a new landscape (p. 5).

16 Korom, for instance, in arguing a case for 'creolization' as an 'apt agency to account for the newly emergent and complex forms of culture that develop through a synthetic process of convergence'

contends that 'creolization' (which also entails decreolization) is 'creative accommodation'. This is more than a process of acculturation: it is 'a valid form of resistance to total cultural absorption' (pp. 12–13). Hence Stuart Hall's perception that diasporic traditions 'are inevitably the products of several interlocking histories and cultures, belonging at the same time to several "homes" – and thus to no particular home'. Stuart Hall, 'Culture, Community, Nation', *Cultural Studies* 7:3 (1993), pp. 349–63, p. 362.

17 James C. Conroy and Robert A. Davis, 'Transgression, Transformation and Enlightenment: The Trickster as Poet and Teacher', *Educational Philosophy and Theory* 34:3 (2002), pp. 255–72, p. 256.

18 Houston A. Baker Jr, 'Foreword', in Joyce Jonas, *Anancy in the Great House: Ways of Reading West Indian Fiction*, Contributions in Afro-American and African Studies, Number 136, New York, Westport, Connecticut, London: Greenwood Press, 1999, p. viii.

19 My preference is for 'Anancy' as this, in my view, is more reflective of the negotiation and adaptation that Ananse of Ashanti folklore had undergone in the landscape of the Caribbean (New World). It also underscores the dynamic and ambivalent nature of the trickster. Nanzi is the name employed in the Dutch-speaking Caribbean, especially Curaçao.

20 For a history of Anancy stories in Jamaica see F. G. Cassidy and R. B. Le Page, *Dictionary of Jamaican English*, New York: Cambridge University Press, 1967; Martha W. Beckwith, *Jamaica Anansi Stories*, New York: American Folklore Society, 1924; Philip Sherlock, *Anansi, the Spider Man*, London: MacMillan, 1959.

21 Jonas, *Anancy in the Great House*, p. 51.

22 Jonas, *Anancy in the Great House*, p. 51.

23 While Anancy is pictured as a male in Caribbean folklore and literature, it is my intention to break this patriarchal stereotype. Anancy, in this volume, may be male, female, transgendered, and may embrace a multiplicity of ethnic identities. She may take the form of human, animal or insect. In other words, unpredictability and ambivalence will be key characteristics of my Anancy.

24 Robert D. Pelton, *The Trickster in West Africa: A Study of Mythic Irony and Sacred Delight*, Berkeley, Los Angeles, London: University of California Press, 1980, p. 35.

25 Diane J. Austin-Broos, *Jamaica Genesis: Religion and Politics of Moral Orders*, Chicago and London: University of Chicago Press, 1997, pp. 47–9.

26 Austin-Broos, *Jamaica Genesis*, pp. 28–9.

27 Austin-Broos, *Jamaica Genesis*, p. 37.

Notes

28 Edward K. Brathwaithe, 'Ananse', in *The Arrivants: A New World Triology*, London: Oxford University Press, 1973, pp. 165–7.

29 Pascale De Souza, 'Creolizing Anancy: Signifyin(g) Processes in New World Spider Tales', in Gordon Collier and Ulrich Fleischmann (eds), *A Pepper-Pot of Cultures: Aspects of Creolization in the Caribbean*, Amsterdam and New York: Rodopi, 2003, pp. 339–40.

30 De Souza, 'Creolizing Anancy'; Jonas, *Anancy in the Great House*; Pelton, *Trickster in West Africa*.

31 See, Andrew Salkey, *Anancy's Score*, London: Bogle-L'Ouverture Publications, 1973.

32 De Souza, 'Creolizing Anancy', p. 340.

33 Pelton, *Trickster in West Africa*, p. 60.

34 Korom, *Hosay Trinidad*, p. 200. Here Korom is making a similar point about the *Hosay* ritual that travelled from India with the indentured Indians who were Muslims.

35 I am aware of the distinction that is often made between 'storytelling' and 'narrative'. It has been suggested that 'narrative' is usually the choice for scholars inclined towards the adult world of power, influence and overt intellectualization. These scholars would rarely use the term 'storytelling', which the practitioners and scholars of 'storytelling' will contend is a method in its own right. This is precisely the point that the editors of the inaugural issue of the journal *Storytelling, Self, Society* make. Contending that storytelling employs the totality of the human person – memory, imagination, emotion, intellect, language, gesture, movement, expression and relationship in the living moment – the editorial sees its task as that of bringing the *logos* (domain of rationality) and the *eros* (domain of emotion, relatedness and spirituality) together. In using these terms interchangeably, I am underscoring the point that through the Anancy paradigm these boundaries become amorphous and unnecessary.

36 These include Ancient Greece, Africa, the Middle East, Asia, the Americas, the Caribbean and Europe. See Paul Radin, *The Trickster: A Study in American Mythology*, New York: Greenwood Press, 1956 and Paul Williams, *The Fool and the Trickster*, Totowa, NJ: Rowman and Littlefield, 1979.

37 James Cone, *God of the Oppressed*, Minneapolis, Minnesota: The Seabury Press, 1977, p. 29.

38 For more on the trickster figure see Barbara Babcock-Abrahams, 'A "Tolerated Margin of Mess": The Trickster and his Tales Reconsidered', *Journal of the Folklore Institute* 11 (1975), pp. 147–86; Laura Makarius, 'Ritual Clowns and Symbolic Behaviour', in *Diogenes* 69 (1970), pp. 44–73; Pelton, *Trickster in West Africa*; Radin, *The Trickster*; Laura Tanna, 'Anansi – Jamaica's

Trickster Hero', in *Jamaica Journal* 16:2 (May 1983), pp. 20–31; Williams, *Fool and the Trickster*.

39 Note the relationship between the trickster qualities and the themes of laughter, absurdity, parody, the carnivalesque and social inversion found in the works of Mikhail Bhaktin and Wilson Harris.

40 Jonas, *Anancy in the Great House*, p. 50.

41 Conroy and Davis, 'Transgression, Transformation and Enlightenment', p. 256.

42 Pelton, *Trickster in West Africa*, p. 260.

43 Pelton, *Trickster in West Africa*, p. 272.

44 Jonas, *Anancy in the Great House*, p. 51.

45 Susan Niditch, *A Prelude to Biblical Folklore: Underdogs and Tricksters*, Chicago: University of Illinois Press, 2000, p. xvi.

46 Niditch, *Prelude to Biblical Folklore*, p. xi. See also, Christiano Grottanelli, 'Tricksters, Scapegoats, Champions, Saviours', in *History of Religions* 23/2 (1983), pp. 117–39; Naomi Steinberg, 'Israelite Tricksters: Their Analogues and Cross-Cultural Study', in *Semeia* 42 (1988), pp. 1–13.

47 Melissa Jackson, 'Lot's Daughters and Tamar as Tricksters and the Patriarchal Narratives as Feminist Theology', *Journal for the Study of the Old Testament* 98 (2002), pp. 29–46. Here Jackson expands on the work of Ann W. Engar, 'Old Testament Women as Tricksters', in Vincent L. Tollers and John Maier (eds), *Mappings of the Biblical Terrain: The Bible as Text*, Lewisburg: Buckness University Press, 1990, pp. 143–57.

48 Niditch, *Prelude to Biblical Folklore*, p. 49.

49 See Sharon D. Welch, *After Empire: The Art and Ethos of Enduring Peace*, Minneapolis: Fortress Press, 2004, p. 56. Welch in her discourse on the trickster draws on the work of Jace Weaver, *Other Worlds: American Indian Literature, Law and Cultures*, Norman: University of Oaklahoma Press, 2001.

50 Welch, *After Empire*, p. 38.

51 See Salkey, *Anancy's Score*, 1973.

52 Shane Phelan, 'Coyote Politics: Trickster Tales and Feminist Futures', *Hypatta* 111:3 (Summer 1996), pp. 130–49.

53 Wendy Doniger, *The Implied Spider: Politics and Theology in Myth*, New York: Columbia University Press, 1998, p. 3.

54 This is a key point that runs throughout the work of the Caribbean writer Wilson Harris (*Tradition, the Writer and Society*, 1973). See also, Conroy and Davis, 'Transgression, Transformation and Enlightenment', p. 263 for a similar, but not necessarily a new insight.

55 See Anthony G. Reddie, *Faith Stories and the Experience of*

Black Elders, London: Jessica Kingsley, 2001. The author argues a case for unearthing and re-surfacing the stories of Black people in the UK.

56 In the tradition of Ada María Isasi-Díaz's articulation of *Mujerista Theology* (see note 4).

57 For example: religion, thought patterns, cultural practices, oral tradition, literature, arts and symbols, etc.

58 Marion Grau argues similarly for the role of the trickster. See Grau, 'Divine Commerce', in Catherine Keller, Michael Nausner and Myra Riveria (eds), *Postcolonial Theologies: Divinity and Empire*, St Louis, Missouri: Chalice Press, 2004, pp. 164–85.

59 Cf. Welch, *After Empire*, pp. 66–7.

60 Cf. Gustavo Gutiérrez, *A Theology of Liberation*, Maryknoll, NY: Orbis, 1988; *We Drink from Our Own Wells*, Maryknoll, NY: Orbis, 1984; Sallie McFague, *Models of God: Theology for an Ecological Nuclear Age*, Philadelphia: Fortress Press, 1998. Most of the liberation, Black, Asian, feminist and womanist theologians underscore this point.

61 Cf. Walter Brueggemann, *Finally Comes the Poet*, Minneapolis: Fortress Press, 1989.

62 See *History of the Voice: The Development of Nation Language in Anglophone Caribbean Poetry*, London: New Beacon, 1984, p. 13. Brathwaithe defines 'nation language' as the submerged area of that dialect which is more closely allied to the African aspect of experience in the Caribbean. In order to survive the weight of New World domination, the mother culture (Africa for Brathwaithe) had to go underground as part of the process to endure the imposition of dominant Eurocentric culture. When it did resurface it embodied visually different forms but was still rooted in the sensibility of the mother culture.

63 For more on this notion of 'space' see the work of Ada María Isasi-Díaz, *Mujerista Theology*. She writes: 'In many ways the utopia that is created by our *mujerista* struggle is not a different place but a different space, a space often assigned to us by the dominant group in society, but also space we have been able to clear for ourselves and inhabit in the midst of a very oppressive place – today's USA society. This space is not an abstraction but rather a spatio-temporal reality that we create in order to have the freedom to envision our preferred future' (p. 164).

64 See Harris, *Explorations* and Gilkes, *Literate Imagination*.

65 Cf. Isasi-Díaz, *La Lucha Continues*, pp. 157–62.

66 Edouard Glissant, *Le Discours Antillais*, Paris: Editions du Seuil, 1980.

67 In using the term 'resistance', I wish to note some of the limitations related to its use as highlighted by Jenny Sharpe in *Ghosts of
Slavery: A Literary Archaeology of Black Women's Lives*, Minneapolis/
London: University of Minnesota Press, 2003. Sharpe notes the
following: 1) While the term suggests antislavery activity it does not
necessarily offer an explanation of ways in which slaves sought to
improve their conditions even though the resistance was not an attack
on the system; 2) When the term is equated 'with an oppositional consciousness' it becomes problematic as this can only be inferred; and
3) The category of resistance loses its meaning with the 'need to identify resistance in even the most accommodating of practices'. Sharpe's
point is that while the category of 'resistance' is helpful as a tool
for collective agency, its importance becomes problematic when
expanded to embrace individual acts. Sharpe's preference is for the
category of 'tactic' (pp. xv–xxi).

68 Vincent L. Wimbush, 'Introduction', in *Rhetorics of Resist-
ance: A Colloquy on Early Christianity as Rhetorical Formation*.
Guest Editor: Vincent L. Wimbush. Board Editor: Sheila Briggs.
Semeia 79 (Society for Biblical Literature, 1997), pp. 1–10, p. 6.

69 James C. Scott, *Domination and the Arts of Resistance:
Hidden Transcripts*, New Haven and London: Yale University Press,
1990, p. xii.

70 Scott, *Domination*, pp. 19–28.

71 *Midrash* means to 'seek out' or 'to inquire'. It is used in a dual
way to describe a method and a genre of literature in which the imagination is used extensively in the interpretation and reinterpretation of
biblical texts to release and extend the texts to existential experiences.

72 I understand boundary as more than the perception of where
things separate. I perceive boundary as the edge or margin where
things join and assume new shapes.

73 Idris Hamid, *In Search of New Perspectives*, Barbados:
CADEC, 1973, p. 8.

74 A. Sivanandan, 'The Liberation of the Black Intellectual' in
Kwesi Owusu (ed.), *Black British Culture and Society: A Text
Reader*, Routledge: London and New York, 2000, pp. 70–81.

75 Derek Walcott, 'A Far Cry from Africa', in *In a Green Night*,
London: Cape, 1962.

76 Walcott, 'A Far Cry', p. 74. This subversion is quite evident
in the literary works of John Agard, Louise Bennett, Kamau
Brathwaithe, Olive Senior, Derek Walcott, among others.

77 Henry Louis Gates Jr, *The Signifying Monkey: A Theory of
Afro-American Literary Criticism*, New York: Oxford University
Press, 1988, p. 52.

78 As quoted by Troy Wilson Organ, *Third Eye Philosophy: Essays in East-West Thought*, Athens, Ohio, London: Ohio University Press, 1987, p. 12.

79 Organ, *Third Eye Philosophy*, p. 54.

80 See John Agard, *Mangoes and Bullets: Selected and New Poems 1972–1984*, London and Sydney: Pluto Press, 1985.

81 De Souza, 'Creolizing Anancy', p. 346.

82 cf. Antonia McDonald-Smythe, '*Kwik! Kwak!* Narrating the Self: A Reading of *The Autobiography of My Mother*', in *Journal of West Indian Literature*, 8:1 (October 1998), pp. 41–55.

83 Hans Reudi-Weber, *The Book that Reads Me*, Geneva: World Council of Churches, 1995.

84 Bronwyn T. Williams, 'A State of Perpetual Wandering: Diaspora and Black British Writers', in *Jouvert* 3:3, 1999), pp. 1–16, p. 2.

85 Cf. works of Caryl Phillips, Hanif Kureishi and Sunetra Gupta, *inter alia*. As cited by Bronwyn Williams.

86 Harvey Cox, *The Feast of Fools: A Theological Essay on Festivity and Fantasy*, Cambridge, Massachusetts: Harvard University Press, 1969.

87 Harvey Cox, *Feast of Fools*, p. 16.

88 Harvey Cox, *Feast of Fools*, pp. 140–1.

89 Harvey Cox, *Feast of Fools*, p. 145.

90 Harvey Cox, *Feast of Fools*, p. 144.

91 Gerard Aching, *Masking Power: Carnival and Popular Culture in the Caribbean*, Minneapolis: University of Minnesota Press, 2002. Cultural Studies Series of the Americas. Edited by George Yúdice, Jean Franco and Juan Flores, p. 32.

92 Grau, 'Divine Commerce', pp. 164–85

93 Grau, 'Divine Commerce', p. 165.

94 Grau, 'Divine Commerce', p. 177.

95 This is with particular reference to Homi Bhabha's *The Location of Culture*, London and New York: Routledge, 1994.

96 Grau, 'Divine Commerce', p. 166.

97 Grau, 'Divine Commerce', p. 168.

98 Bhabha, *Location of Culture*, pp. 121 and 86.

99 Grau, 'Divine Commerce', p. 177.

100 Grau, 'Divine Commerce', p. 184.

101 Sallie McFague, *Metaphorical Theology*, Philadelphia: Fortress Press, 1982, p. 17.

102 See also, C. S. Song, *The Compassionate God: An Exercise in the Theology of Transposition*, London: SCM Press, 1982; *Theology from the Womb of Asia*, London: SCM Press, 1982.

103 See Fred D'Aguiar, 'Home is Always Elsewhere: Individual and Regenerative Capacities of Loss' in Owusu, *Black British Culture and Society*, pp. 195–206.

104 See, 'The Hitchhikers', in *Beyond the River*, Auckland: Ashton Scholastic, 1994, for Joy Cowley's use of storyteller as a thief, magician, seamstress and liberator.

105 Insights from Agard, *Mangoes and Bullets*, pp. 27–8.